Color Me Included clears the fogge ... ... ui a long-overlooked chapter in the history of Hampton and her daughter towns. General readers and researchers alike will enjoy this thoughtful, comprehensive, and well-researched book on the area's early African American population.

—**Cheryl Lassiter, author of** *The Mark of Goody Cole: a tragic and true tale of witchcraft persecution in the history of early America*

This is local history at its finest. Deborah Knowlton has done an outstanding job in this well researched, well written, and highly interesting book bringing forth the life details of those individuals who lived their lives in the shadows of history.

—**Glenn A. Knoblock, historian and author of** *Strong and Brave Fellows; New Hampshire's Black Soldiers and Sailors of the American Revolution, 1775-1784*

Knowlton has painstakingly recovered extensive information about the lives of colonial and early nineteenth-century African Americans from Hampton and coastal New Hampshire. Now more than ever, it is essential for all Americans to understand the impact of African Americans on our early history, and this book demonstrates the often significant roles African Americans played in Congregational churches, the New England economy, and military campaigns, including the American Revolution. Despite racism and slavery, Knowlton correctly shows that these men and women made choices for themselves and their children by participating (or not) in churches, by running away from slavery, or by seeking freedom though other means. This book joins the small but growing list of histories that enrich our understanding of the complicated connections between race relations and religion in America.

—**Richard J. Boles, Ph.D., Historian, The City College of New York.**

Color Me Included is full of surprises. It exposes centuries-old family secrets with respectful compassion while not romanticizing the unknowable, describing "unnamed negroes" as actual human beings that had been captured, bought and inherited as taxable property by generations of enslavers who, otherwise, we thought we knew so well. Also, the complicity of non-slaveholders in the eighteenth century slave-based economy becomes abundantly clear. Fascinating stories introduce some of the individual Black people who can be traced in public records, "ironically," as the author points out, because the ruling class documented African Americans who were enslaved but not those who were free. With emancipation came relentlessly challenging forms of rejection, forcing able-bodied free people out of the small towns of New Hampshire. No longer needed, their former presence was quickly forgotten. Quoting the author again, "Sometimes what is in the record is the most surprising truth of all."

—Valerie Cunningham, Founder of The Portsmouth Black Heritage Trail, community historian, preservationist, and co-author of the book, *Black Portsmouth: Three Centuries of African American Heritage*

Color Me Included

Color Me Included

*The African Americans of
Hampton's First Church and Its
Descendant Parishes, 1670-1826*

By

Deborah B. Knowlton, M.Div.

Peter E. Randall Publisher
Portsmouth, New Hampshire
2016

Peter E. Randall Publisher
Box 4726
Portsmouth, New Hampshire, 03802
www.perpublisher.com

ISBN: 978-1-937721-28-2
Library of Congress Control Number: 2016930073

Book design by Grace Peirce

Cover illustration by Maggie Ginieres
Unless otherwise noted all photographs by
Veronica Wichrowski

I dedicate this book to the African Americans of First Congregational Church and its related church communities. Discovering their lives and telling their stories has changed forever how I imagine the beloved community. Such a community cannot happen as a result of political or economic ends. Neither can it be created by laws or ideologies. It is only through telling and listening to our different stories that we truly discover how to live with and love each other. May their stories serve to bend the arc of history ever so slightly toward a more lively and inclusive spirit of brotherhood and sisterhood.

Contents

Preface

"When I think of slavery it makes me mad. I do not believe in giving you my story, 'cause with all the promises that have been made, the Negro is still in a bad way in the United States, no matter in what part he lives. It's all the same. Now you may be all right; there're a few white men who are, but the pressure is such from your white friends that you will be compelled to talk against us and give us the cold shoulder when you are around them, even if your heart is right towards us."

—Thomas Hall, Interviewed by T. Pat Matthews, Sept 10, 1937, for the *WPA Slave Narrative Project, North Caroline Narratives*, vol. 11, part 1.

THIS BOOK WAS WRITTEN to bring to light the lives and conditions of the forgotten people of color who were part of the First Congregational Church of Hampton, New Hampshire, faith community during its first two centuries.

Most of the material used to discover the names of African Americans who were baptized, married, or became members of the First Congregational Church was found in three volumes of church records that were not publicly available in their entirety prior to this research. The three volumes used were entitled "Volume I & II," "Volume 2," and "Volume 3." They are each handwritten bound volumes that were copied from original records. The description below shows the years that these volumes cover and what records were available from Rev. Seaborn Cotton's ministry, which began in 1657, through to Rev. J. A. Ross's ministry, which ended in 1902. The Hampton

Historical Society, in cooperation with the First Congregational Church, is in the process of making digital copies of these works for those who may want to do further research on this or other topics of church history.

Included in these records are the names of persons who joined the church, were baptized, married, and died. Regular church meeting minutes that cover a wide range of church business—including decisions from hiring pastors to who must be dismissed for breaking the seventh commandment—are included as well. The majority of African-American names are listed between the years 1700 and 1820.

The complete list of what each of the three bound volumes includes is listed below:

Volume I & II: 1657–1765
- Copied from original records
- Fragmentary Records of Rev. Seaborn Cotton (1657–1686) as copied by Rev. John Cotton, pages 1–6
- Records of Rev. John Cotton (1696–1710), pages 7–58
- Records of Rev. Nathaniel Gookin (1710–1734), pages 60–173
- A portion of Records of Rev. Ward Cotton, 1765, pages 174–300

Volume 2: 1756–1840
- Copied from Original Books 2 and 3
- Continued Records of Rev. Ward Cotton, pages 1-84, 198-204, 257-262
- Records of Rev. Ebenezer Thayer, pages 85-171, 204-214, 262-272
- Records of Jesse Appleton, pages 174-179, 217-220, 273-276
- Records of Josiah Webster, pages 180-195, 221-254, 277-280

Volume 3: 1808–1902

- Copied from Original Books 4, 5, 6
- Records of Rev. Josiah Webster, pages 1–95
- Records of Rev. E.D. Eldridge, pages 95–141, 169-174, 189-193
- Records of Rev. S. Payson Fay, pages 143–150, 177-178, 196-198, 220-221
- Records of Rev. J. Colby, pages 151-155, 179-180, 202-207
- Records of Rev. W.W. Fay, pages 156–157, 166, 183-184, 208
- Records of Rev. J.A. Ross, pages 159–166, 185-186, 212-217
- Presbyterian Records, pages 271–286

Volumes I & II, 2, and 3 of the First Congregational Church Records, containing Deaths, Baptisms, Marriages and Church Meeting Minutes from the years 1657 to 1902. Photo courtesy of Veronica Wichrowski.

I began a search in 2013, in the 375th anniversary year of the founding of First Congregational Church. I wanted to know how closely, if at all, that first faith community resembled the worshiping body of the twenty-first century. I wondered what the earliest congregation had looked like. How many men were members and how many women? Did children appear in the record? Might there have been members with mixed ethnic backgrounds? How diverse was that first faith community? This last question became much more focused and intriguing when I began to discover African American slaves who are identified in Record Book I and II for the First Congregational Church of Hampton, New Hampshire. I noted a dozen or more Africans listed as having been baptized or joined as members. I realized that with the number of names listed indicating African and even Native American ancestry, that the congregation of the early eighteenth century was far more diverse than the present-day faith community. I decided to learn more about these early members, some of whom were slaves, others indentured servants, and still others, free men and women of color. Their stories are not mine to tell except through a desire on my part to acknowledge their contributions as ancestors and founders of the town of Hampton and of the First Congregational Church. "They" are "us" whether they are named or not, whether there is one line to their life's story that has survived or whether several generations can be traced. I undertake with great care the telling of the stories that follow of slaves or servants. I tell their tales hoping that my heart is right toward all and my shoulders are squared so I might look and see them, perhaps for the first time as builders of the town of Hampton and spiritual ancestors of the parish that has continuously gathered for worship in the heart of its town for more than three centuries.

The African Americans included in *Color Me Included* were not always given a name nor identified with their owner, especially if they had already been freed. However, where possible, African Americans are listed by as much of their own name as is known followed by the family name of their owner in parentheses. This method is meant to help identify family connections, as persons were dismissed from First Congregational Church and new parishes and towns were founded.

For purposes of this historical sketch of Hampton, New Hampshire, the term, "African American," is used throughout to broadly describe those who were enslaved and those who lived as free blacks in the community. In most cases, the record books that were accessed offered no details about the birth places of those listed. This phrase, while less than accurate, is meant to reflect the fact that the majority of slaves who came to New England between 1670 and 1826, came by way of the Triangle trade and likely came from West Africa and remained in America until their deaths.

One quick word about dates—prior to 1752, Great Britain used the Julian calendar. The switch to the Gregorian calendar involved several changes including changing the start of the New Year from March 25 to January 1. In cases where the original date listed in the church records may cause confusion to contemporary readers—mostly for dates between January 1 and March 24—I have added the "current" year second, for example, February 1714/1715 would have originally been in the year 1714 that ended in March but would now be in the year 1715 that would have begun by our reckoning in January. This is helpful to keep in mind when calculating ages for individuals whose lives include the year the calendar was changed.

Acknowledgments

AS A FIRST-TIME AUTHOR, I received support, helpful criticism, and sincere encouragement for which I am deeply thankful. Elizabeth Aykroyd and Bill Teschek encouraged me from the beginning. They each gave me hints about where to start my research, and both read early manuscripts. Cheryl Lassiter and Glenn Knoblock have offered historical, grammatical, and artistic help; and, as authors themselves, have shown great generosity and wisdom in helping me think out loud about how best to lift up untold stories. Members of the Hampton Historical Society, as well as other state and area library and historical staff, have helped finding sources and locating family histories and gave freely of their time and enthusiasm. Richard Boles encouraged me to look for original sources with care and diligence whenever possible. Valerie Cunningham offered support amidst a busy season in her life by her willingness to read my manuscript with suggestions in mind. Maggie Ginieres created and presented me with the book's cover sketch. Veronica Wichrowski freely shared her time and talent as a photographer. Family and friends have encouraged me from the start, and I thank especially Maren and Donald Tirabassi, Jean Bass, Charles Burwell, and my children, Sarah and Daniel Knowlton. They believed in me, but more importantly, they celebrated the need for lifting up African-American life stories, unknown or forgotten, that were worthy of thanksgiving and honor.

CHAPTER 1
....

How African Americans Came to Reside
in Hampton, New Hampshire

THE SLAVE TRADE, ESPECIALLY from Africa, was already over one hundred years old when the first Dutch ship landed twenty Africans at Jamestown Colony in 1619. Of course, if we look well back in history, we recognize evidence of a slave trade in even the most ancient of cultures. Slavery under the Pharaoh was the ancient curse of the Hebrew people and the freeing of them God's most precious act of mercy on their behalf.[1]

In New Hampshire, slavery came as it did in other New England colonies. It came as the first towns began to be settled and the need for labor grew. After all, there was land to clear, crops to plant and harvest and homes, shops and meeting-houses to build. African slaves were noted in New Hampshire by 1645—a full twenty-five years after the Dutch ship landed in Virginia. Perhaps because New Hampshire did not impose a tariff on slaves, more landed first in New Hampshire and then were sold into other colonies. Because it was New Hampshire's largest seaport, slaves were settled first in and around Portsmouth. In 1682, correspondence between Virginia's William Fitzhugh and the Cutts family of Portsmouth included

1

negotiations concerning the purchase of slaves in exchange for tobacco.

Shortly before these negotiations, in May of 1680, Governor Simon Bradstreet sent a letter to the Committee of Trade and Plantations in England. It was meant to answer twenty-seven inquiries from the committee regarding the state and condition of the colony. Since New Hampshire was a part of the Massachusetts Colony until 1680, the conditions queried would also have applied to Hampton. The governor's response indicated to the committee that there were nearly twenty English merchant traders who frequented the colony's port. These merchants, said Bradstreet, went to Carolina and places less inhabited since much of the land along the seacoast had already been appropriated and the taming of the country to the north of Boston and inland was much more difficult. He said:

> . . . no company of blacks has been brought here for 50 years from the beginning of the plantation but one small vessel arrived two years since after 20 months voyage from Madagascar with 40 or 50 negroes mostly women or children who sold for 10, 15 or 20 pounds...now and then 2 to 3 negroes are brought hither from Barbadoes or other English plantations and sold for about 20 pounds apiece so that there may be in the government only about 120 persons making up the entire slave population in all of Massachusetts....not above 5 or 6 blacks born in a year, none baptised; about 400 or 500 whites born one year and another, most baptised except those who do not desire it.[2]

There were at least some early attempts at emancipation. It was reported that, "Isaac Morrill, a native of New Jersey came to Newbury in March of 1690, to entice Indians and Negroes to leave their masters and go with him, saying that the English should be cut off, and the negroes should be free."[3] Morrill was arrested May 29 and sent to Ipswich for trial. The results of the trial are unknown, but his plan was to sail a ship from Newbury to Canada to join with the French against the English, saving none but Negroes and Indians. Then he would return over the Merrimac River, by Archelaus Hill on the backside of John Emery's meadow to destroy Haverhill and Amesbury. Morrill's early anti-bondage rhetoric is evident a mere forty-five years after the first slaves were imported to New Hampshire.

Judge Sewall, a Massachusetts printer and businessman, wrote, in 1710, a tract against slavery titled *The Selling of Joseph.*"[4] Elihu Coleman, a Quaker living in Nantucket who was a neighbor of Christopher Hussey, also wrote a signature tract calling for the end of slavery.[5] Both of these were written just twenty years after Isaac Morrill's plot to free Negroes failed because of his arrest. Neither tract gained much notice at the time, but it seems that between the end of the seventeenth century and the midpoint of the eighteenth century the sentiment toward slave owning in New England had already begun to shift. This shift would become dramatic following the end of the Revolutionary War, as soldiers returned to their homes and towns with slaves who had fought beside them in battles and skirmishes across New England. One can only imagine the conversations between owners returning as newly freed colonists and their African and West Indian compatriots, still in bondage. Such conversations would have been worth recording.

In Old Hampton, as in any village or agrarian hamlet, there is always a season and a time for every purpose under heaven. Slave holding had begun in the late seventeenth century, peaked in the mid-eighteenth and was hardly noticeable in New Hampshire by the late 1790s. Only three persons appear in the town records of Hampton identified as slaves prior to 1700:

Shirk, Negro Jack, and an unnamed black teenager bought of Mr. Pottle. By 1713, it is estimated that perhaps one hundred Negro slaves were living in New Hampshire; by the 1730s that number was nearly two hundred slaves with about one-third of them living in Portsmouth.

Between 1736 and 1790, about twenty names are recorded in the church record—ten times the number of slaves recorded prior to 1700. Statewide, in this same period, the number of slaves recorded also jumped from two hundred to five hundred. In the 1730s a simple survey was done in an attempt to esti-mate the number of families owning at least three to four slaves. Forty families were estimated to own that number of slaves in Portsmouth, fifteen in Exeter, five in Hampton Falls and four families in Hampton. Such a rise was due to a kind of clustering of slaves and slave owners along seacoast areas where trading and wealth formation, culture and politics had first taken root. It also reflects the increased acreage in farming and the need for a larger work force.

With this rise in numbers of slaves, there does not seem to have been a simultaneous rise in violence against them. Just prior to 1700, the General Assembly passed a law that provided the penalty of being whipped with stripes not to exceed twenty for anyone who received stolen goods from any "Indian, Mulatto, Negro Servant or Slave, or other known, dissolute, lewd, or disorderly person of whom there is just cause of suspi-cion" if such goods were not returned or redress made. This law was followed in 1714/1715 with laws that forbade servants or Negroes from drinking at a local tavern without their master's consent or of creating disorders in the night. In fact, a 9:00 p.m. curfew on all non-white slaves or servants was imposed because: "great Disorders, Insolvencies and Burglaries are oft-times Raised and Committed in the Night time by Indians, Negroes and Molatto Servants and Slaves to the Disquiet and Hurt of her Majesties good Subjects."[6] These few laws are the only ones enacted before 1760 that relate to African Americans living in New Hampshire. No new laws were written in the 1730s and '40s when the importation of slaves increased tremendously.

The faith of many African Americans was an important resource in their continual stretch toward freedom. They did not fail to hear the persistent message in the mouth of Jesus, the teacher, who told His listeners that God loves all human beings equally. In 1773, a group of blacks petitioned the legislature of Massachusetts for their freedom and justified the unrighteousness of slavery with words of faith: "We have no property! We have no wives! No children! We have no city! No country! But we have a Father in Heaven, and we are determined, as far as his Grace shall enable us, and as far as our degraded contemptuous life will admit, to keep all his Commandments."[7]

Just prior to the Revolutionary War and immediately afterward, slave owners began to free their slaves in ever increasing numbers. To look at this decrease in the number of owned slaves living in New Hampshire in yet one more way, we note that in 1715, the first general census of New England's population was taken. The results reported counted 4,150 "negroes" or about one Negro for every six white families.[8] In 1775, there were living in Hampton a total of 862 persons of whom three were Negroes and slaves for life. A list compiled shortly thereafter of men who served in the Revolution from Hampton includes the names of African-American soldiers George Long, Caesar Clough, and Cato Moulton, as well as other African Americans who were paid for duty at Ticonderoga, such as Paul Long and Caesar Small.[9] All of these men we will meet later in this work.

The 1790 general census showed only 97 Negro slaves in all of New Hampshire (also 292 free, non-white others) among a total population of 43,185 persons. In 1790, the states of Vermont and Massachusetts (which included Maine until 1820) were reporting no slaves held at all. We need to remember, however, that this census was the first time any complete accounting of persons was undertaken. One can see that without good roads into certain small neighborhoods, for example, census takers could easily have missed persons, especially those still enslaved. In fact, when the 1790 census results were tallied from the very beginning, President Washington was surprised that the totals came in under what he'd imagined. Regardless of possible census reporting issues, it is clear that numbers of slaves owned had declined significantly in seventy-five years' time. This decline of the slave population continued well after the Revolutionary battle for freedom and liberty was over. The Revolutionary battle put into perspective the new paradigm that all men were created equal. This meant free from colonial impe-rialism and free from the immorality of slave-holding. By 1840 there were only twenty-three owned slaves listed in all of the six New England states.[10]

Why There Was a Perceived Need for Slave-holding in Hampton

If the Hampton church records are a window on the culture of the early eighteenth century, then it is evident that although a wide range of duties were certainly performed by slaves, by the time of the Revolution, most were still owned by shipping merchants, doctors, ministers and public officials. It may be easy to conclude that the more wealth a family had, the greater the ability to purchase someone to do the hard and dangerous tasks for them. In this case, it might be easy to see slave-holding as a sign of wealth and status. However, all of these occupations also demanded long hours away from the household. Clergy were often called away for visits, preaching circuits and collegial duties on behalf of other pastors and parishes. So, too, politicians often were away for months at a time, as were ship captains and even doctors who traveled great distances to perform medical procedures for their neighbors. This left the women and children of such households without significant help from the head of the household in producing the harvest needed for survival.

Slavery allowed not only help with the survival of individual families but supported a growing economy beyond what each household consumed. Excess fish, eggs, apples, and timber gained by slave labor could transform a family from consumers to retailers.

As the culture grew more aware of the costs of production, internal conflict about how this production was to be accomplished may have increased. Perhaps some of these dynamics are represented in another law that came in 1728. The law stated that each slave holder would be taxed a certain amount (twenty pounds) for each male Negro or mulatto or Indian slave owned.[11] Is it possible that if citizens declared their ownership of a slave as they would the number of oxen owned, farm implements or acres of land, then the practice of owning a slave would feel more business-like in a perverse way? At least their provenance was declared.

In New Hampshire, as elsewhere, another dynamic was occurring alongside the African slave trade in the early years of the eighteenth century. Some early English settlers had themselves come to New England as indentured servants, agreeing to a limited number of years of bonded work in exchange for food and lodging until they could become more independent. Other settlers had turned to prisoners or debtors from England and Ireland as a source of additional labor. These whites were named "indentured servants" and were, for the most part, freed after several years. If such servants chose to flee before their bond was complete, they sometimes changed their names or settled in a different place. Their ability to do so was much easier than it was for African Americans because of skin color.

During 1740–1746, so many children were kidnapped from Aberdeen, Scotland, that parents grew fearful of even sending their children on a local errand.[12] Most of those kidnapped were children who were auctioned off at the wharfs, their names recorded along with the length of their indenture. Many needed years of growth to become strong enough to do the kind of work the early colonists needed to accomplish in order to survive.

In the early years of the eighteenth century, this practice of public indenture was part of the social contract in many New England colonies. On the surface, it may have appeared similar to apprenticing someone as a means for them to learn a skill. But Ruth Wallis Herndon, in a work regarding indenture, argues that public indenture of white persons was essentially a solution to the social problem of the costs associated with maintaining the poor.[13]

Slavery was something entirely different. A slave had no contract and no expectation of eventual economic, social, or political independence. The social relationship itself was different from indenture. Instead of eventually obtaining independence, African slaves' rights of productivity, reproduction, labor, and personhood were assigned to another person. This shift in who benefited in the marketplace, if you will, meant that a slave received no benefits. Rather the social contract with slaves led to kinlessness, objectification, and exclusion, not just for the length of a contract, but for a length whose end might never be determined.[14]

One author uses the term "double consciousness" to describe the attitude that developed between a white slave owner of faith and a black slave being tutored in the faith. On the one hand, the slave owner wants to offer the slave an opportunity for spiritual conversion if not redemption. On the other hand, the

African American or Native American man, woman, or child is considered a commodity or possession. Is it reasonable to wish redemption for a commodity? Could a person be sub-human and yet sanctified into the image of God; a fellow brother or sister in Christ and at the same time an "other" who could be kidnapped, bought, and sold at will? Such juxtapositions meant that within the worship setting there resided the chance that the image of God might prevail on the Sabbath and include the images of black slaves. Monday morning, however, when business deals were made, the inferior nature of the "other" was all too evident in the expectations of owners that these Christian slaves be diligent to the owners, patient with their "station" and mindful about any act or word that might displease.

CHAPTER 2

The Puritan Church and Slavery

THE PURITAN FAITH COMMUNITY theoretically considered their slaves to be part of the Puritan household and a part of the Puritan covenant. This covenant between themselves, the land, and their God resembled the early covenants that God made with the Israelites when Abraham and Sarah received land and descendants more numerous than the stars.[1] Early New England Puritans attached a great deal of importance to New England land ownership, because they believed God had granted this gift as if it were the new "promised land." In fact, Cotton Mather wrote often as if the history of New England and the history of Israel were to be read as one interwoven story. God, he believed, destined the Puritans to settle in New England, to subdue it, and have dominion over it just as Abraham, Isaac, and Jacob subdued the Canaanite inhabitants who lived in the land promised to them. New England's towns, one-by-one, became new Jerusalems of this land. Although in theory Puritans believed that their slaves were part of the covenant elect, in actuality, they were left out of the great covenant destiny, just as certain Israelites had been left out of the first biblical covenant. Even as the earliest religious holiness codes of Exodus[2] prohibited those with maladies or diseases and those tormented in mind or spirit from worshiping in the inner porch of the Jerusalem temple, so, too, did the earliest Puritan colonists exclude Africans in the fullness of the promises of these new "cities on a hill."

Puritanism dominated the religious practices and politics of the New Hampshire seacoast. Hampton founder Rev. Stephen Bachiler and his band of settlers were among the first wave of the "great migration" from England. This migration of religious dissenters began to slow in England about 1641 but by then 21,000 had crossed the Atlantic according to Perry Miller. For the next one hundred years, until the Great Awakening of the 1730s and 1740s in New England, only Hampton, of the four original towns, Portsmouth, Dover, Exeter and Hampton, never developed an appreciable dissent to the Puritan beliefs. As the population grew, in fact doubling between 1700 and 1732, most communities began a push-back against the strict Puritan practices. But in Hampton, things changed more slowly. "In some old church orders for seating, boys were classed with Negroes and seated with them, but in nearly all towns, the Negroes had seats by themselves. The black women were all seated on a long bench or in an enclosed pew labeled 'B.W.' and the Negro men in another labeled, 'B.M.'"[3] Foot stoves were part of the early worshiper's furnishing and often these were carried into church by a black man who, after placing it under his lady's feet, would retire to the balcony or loft where there was no insulation and no heat. The unheated balcony might have served as the "outer porch" of the Jerusalem temple, so to speak.

Seating arrangements, however, were not the only way the church declared its struggle with all persons having equal access to God's covenant of love. While no person, white or black, could truly declare who was predestined by God for salvation or condemnation, the sacraments of baptism and Communion were also limited to those persons who professed their faith, attested to experiencing God's saving grace in their life, and lived an outwardly godly life. In other words, they were only for church members or children of church members. In many Dutch Reformed traditions, only those who had received full membership could be baptized. In 1662, many of the Congregational churches did vote to make baptism a bit more accessible. They voted a Half-way covenant. The Half-way covenant was a change in church policy that lowered the bar for persons who had been baptized but had not become full members to have their children baptized if the parents' behavior was free of scandal, if they publicly adopted the statement of faith associated with baptism, and said they would submit to the discipline of other church members in all things. The First Congregational Church of Hampton records give evidence that the congregation voted to accept the Half-way covenant, but since the records of this moment in the church's history do not exist, we do not have the actual number who voted or the date of the vote.

So, if the seating arrangements, the practices of the rites of Communion, and baptism served to physically separate the white worshipers from the black worshipers, what was the route necessary to proclaim, "That they may all be one?" Thomas Shepard, an early and well-respected Puritan preacher, suggested in a series of sermons that as settlers established each new town in New England and put in place each social institution that God's new creation was coming to fruition. He likened the establishment of New England Protestant churches to the twelve disciples in the Garden of Gethsemane with Jesus who are asked to stay alert. Once the churches felt secure, Shepard asked, would they fall asleep? Would they rely only on the social or cultural ways of ordering community? Would they forget the work that lay before them for the establishment of this new promised land and the creation of a newly covenanted people as God's kingdom on earth? He warned that we must not fall asleep to God's Word, but keep our hearts open to the inward working of the Holy Spirit.[4] The heart, after all, was where God worked, not in the shuffling of persons on the sanctuary floor or around the Communion table.

The Hebrew word *lev,* meaning "heart," includes the emotions such as love and kindness when defining the meaning of heart. "He has a good heart" thus does not mean he has a healthy heart so much as one full of kindness.[5] But the Hebrew faith saw the heart, and not the brain, as the seat of thought. To the ancient Hebrews the heart was the mind—including all thoughts and all desires. When we are told to love God with all our heart (Deut. 6:5), it is an invitation to love with our whole being. The first picture letter in this Hebrew word is a shepherd staff and represents authority as the shepherd has authority over his flock. The second picture letter is of the floor plan of the nomadic tent and represents the idea of being inside as the family resides within the tent. When combined they mean "the authority of the shepherd within." In other words, each human being has within himself or herself the authority within to love, to think, to choose, to belong, and to risk giving their heart's desire away.

It was this "authority within" that I believe prompted the band of Hampton settlers to ignore the Church of England's requests to rethink their radical beliefs. Rather than surrender their "inner authority" to believe as others dictated, they set out for a place where their heart's authority could find free expression. It is this irony—the free of heart, who settled in the new colonies—those who desired the welcome into the shepherd's tent and the name, "family of God" could, it seems, not see to extend this same freedom to those they bought and sold. Was the early colonial church a place where African Americans felt the Spirit's invitation to "step inside the tent of the family of humanity"? Or, was this "sacred space" a reminder that the desire of a slave's heart was still somehow different and the "shepherd's crook" symbol of Christ just one more image of submission?

The answers to these questions are complex. Many of New Hampshire's early Congregational churches could definitely be defined as interracial communities during the period of 1730 to 1820. They were interracial in that different races jointly participated in almost all the religious activities and rituals of these churches.[6] On the surface, such congregations could seem to exemplify the image of a tent large enough for all to be welcome. Numerous Africans and American Indians were baptized along with their children. They cared for persons and were cared for by others under this big tent. They received Communion, listened to sermons, sang Psalms and prayed along with their fellow Caucasian congregants. Having said this, however, does not imply that Africans or Indians received equal treatment. They could not vote in church affairs or hold leadership or pastoral positions. They sat in segregated pews in balconies or pews at the very back of the main sanctuary floor during worship, often relegated to the young lads' pew, implying they were like children. So, the community was interracial, in ways that were sometimes uneasy and in other ways that seemed to work without apparent conflict. But the presence of owned black slaves also gave a clear and constant incentive for reflection on God's dream for "re-membering" God's people. The question that hung in the air and still does, might have been: "How long before our human hearts and minds and strength of will are set on a unity that goes beyond what is visible?"

In the following pages, the hope is two-fold. First, to give as much expression as possible to the lives of those slaves whose names appeared in the journals of the earliest ministers of First Congregational Church of Hampton. Second, to include in more of an overview form, the names of slaves in the towns of Hampton Falls, Kingston, and North Hampton church records; and as these three towns grew, to include the towns of Seabrook, Kensington, Kingston, East Kingston, Sandown, and Danville. The reason for this extension beyond Hampton is that many of the Hampton families who owned slaves moved to one of these "daughter" or granddaughter" towns as Hampton's square acreage was divided again and again to define new town settlements and church starts. As families left in this process of growth and re-location, so, too, did their slaves. As their stories are told, the backdrop is whether or in what ways they fit into the life of their local faith community.

A caution—almost every time an African American is mentioned in the early records, not even the names that are recorded are their own. Rather, the names recorded for them, both first and last, are also reminders of their bondage. First names such as Cromwell, Caesar, or Cato were reminders of the names of sometimes ruthless oppressors. At other times, the first name of a slave may have simply been the name of the ship that brought them to New England such as: *Ann, Jonathan, Nancy, Nanny, Scipio,* or *Sally.* A Caesar in one family may be the same Caesar in another family or a second individual altogether. Only occasionally does a first name seem to reflect some tie to the slave owner's family. For example, Alice Page, is the only Alice listed as a slave in Hampton and Alice was a Page family name.

Slaves' last names were often the names of the family who owned them and, thus, the last names changed as their owner-ship changed. Even in this, we are reminded that in the ancient Hebrew faith, to speak the name of someone meant you held power over that person. For this reason, early, chanted readings of Hebrew scripture always omitted the speaking aloud of the name of God so as never to give the impression that the speaker held "power" over God. What is left of a slave's "inner authority" if not even his or her name is that which was "whispered and known in the womb before you were born"? (Jeremiah 1:5) The hope is to recover in so far as possible both name and, in some rare cases, a glimpse into the inner strength and authority of these men and women whose lives and contributions have, for too long, resided in the shadows. The hope is to re-member!

CHAPTER 3

Hampton's Earliest Known Slaves

R ECORDS DO EXIST CONCERNING slaves who lived with families in towns in or near Hampton prior to 1670. For example, the constable of Ipswich, Massachusetts, was asked to pick up the tavern tab for the jury that was deliberating during the inquest of William Cottle's "Neger" in 1669.[1] Hampton's earliest slave record begins with Shirk, a Negro belonging to Stephen Hussey. This record comes not from the church journal, but from the journal of Captain Henry Dow.

Shirk (Hussey)

The first American-built slave ship, named *Desire*, sailed from Marblehead, Massachusetts, to the west coast of Africa and began to load its cargo of Africans bound for the colonies about the time Hampton was founded in 1638. Rev. Stephen Bachiler, first pastor of the Hampton Congregational Church, left England about 1632 and with a small number of followers settled first in Lynn (first known as Saugus), Massachusetts, where he quickly took up clerical work. After a time, he was asked to leave town due to his extreme ecclesiastical views. He and his band of faithful traveled north, stopping for a while in Newbury, Massachusetts, before ending up in Hampton in 1638.

Since the church does not have more than a few jottings by the early clergy in terms of records, we don't know from early church records if *Desire* brought a load of slaves to Hampton as early as 1640. We also have no indications in the church records of the seventeenth century that any slaves or servants took steps toward participation in any of the sacraments or toward membership in the church earlier than 1736. If they did, their names and any distinguishing adjective to mark them as "free black" or "Negro slave" were not recorded in the first ecclesial records of the church. Hampton town records and personal diaries that survived, as well as court records, occasionally list slaves who were owned prior to 1670, but such records do not reflect church membership or baptismal status.

The Hampton town records, however, do indicate that in 1672, "Shirk, a Negro of Stephen Hussey, was found dead and an inquest held on March, 17, 1671/72."[2] This is an interesting single line of information. It was rare for inquests to be held even on the occasion of the death of an Englishman. They often were held when a body was found washed up on the beach. Why was it then that Shirk's death, one who was simply a slave, resulted in an inquest? Who asked for the inquest? Where had the death occurred and why was it suspicious? We do not know the answers to all of these questions, but certain facts remain as a result of an account of this inquest in Captain Henry Dow's diary that covers the years 1672 until 1702. In that diary Dow's account takes us to the scene as the account begins, "we [the jury] find the Negro dead lying abroad upon his back with one hand stretched out and the other upon his breast."[3]

Looking closely at his body they "could not find any blow nor wound nowhere about his body nor anywhere about him whereby that we can say it was the cause of his death." They even shifted his body, which must have been lying abroad for a while, because when moved, "he purged all the nose." Juror

Will Marston gave witness that, "he came from Piscataqua with [Shirk] the day before and the Negro complained that he was not well but was troubled with pain in his breast."[4] After a careful observation, the jury spoke as one and the verdict was that Shirk had died of natural causes. The members of the jury included Francis Page, who was Will Marston's brother-in-law. Francis was also great-grandfather to Lucy Page, whose daughter, Alice, was a mulatto child. None of the other jurors were men whose families appear in town or church records as slave-owners.

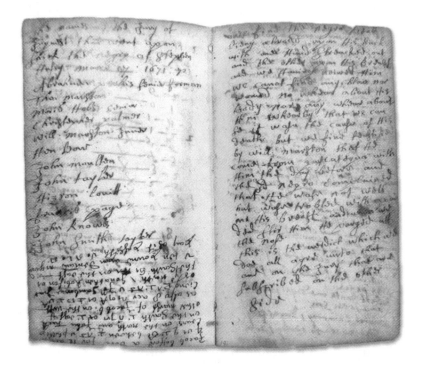

Captain Henry Dow's Diary 1672-1702; An account of the Inquest into Shirk's Death, Courtesy of the Hampton Historical Society Archives.

Stephen Hussey, Shirk's owner, was a grandson of Stephen Bachiler. As a young man, Hussey went to sea. Attracted to the climate and people of Barbados, he settled there for a time and became an official in one of the cities. Many English settlers of his day were buying land for plantation planting and the slave trade was active throughout the West Indies. Hussey was actively involved in this trade. It is quite possible that Hussey bought Shirk in Barbados and brought him back to Hampton. Barbados was also the site of a thriving Quaker community. Stephen Hussey would have found this to his liking since he was drawn to their tenets of faith. But Hussey was not a man of peace as one might imagine a Quaker to be. He was quick to speak his mind and had a strong will and a fiery temper. In April 1668, the Hampton court charged Hussey "for disturbing the congregation on the Lord's Day and reviling Mr. Cotton."[5] Since no love was lost between Congregationalists and Quakers, it may have been Hussey's temper and his religious inclinations that inspired the inquest. Upon Shirk's death, however, it is less important who called for the inquest of a slave, than the fact that a jury of respected town leaders took the time and the care to determine without doubt, that no foul play was involved.

At about the same time as the inquest, in 1671, Christopher Hussey, Stephen's father, gave Stephen a deed to his property on Nantucket Island. Stephen arrived in Nantucket in May of 1673 to manage the Hussey property there in Sherburne. Nantucket Island became Stephen's residence for the rest of his life. From its ports, several of the Hussey men set out in search of whales off the coast. Nantucket whalers were known to call a shark a "sherk" and one wonders whether Hussey ever thought of Shirk, who had been found dead and lying abroad, when he heard the word "shirk" called out from the crow's nest?

After a time, Stephen married Martha Bunker and his probate record indicates that he "gave to his wife, Martha, a

Negro woman, Sarah; to his son, Silvanus, a Negro boy, Mark, to his daughter Theodate, a Negro girl, Dorothy."[6] Only Shirk appears in the Hampton record as belonging to Stephen Hussey and then only at Shirk's death. It is from Stephen's death record that we learn of the Negroes Sarah, Mark, and Dorothy. Were they Shirk's family members, his wife and children? We will never know, but it was very common for African American couples, if they were allowed to marry at all, to remain separated from one another, serving in different households. If children were born, the children often remained with the mother only as long as they were nursing. The record shows that Stephen Hussey owned slaves throughout his life despite his Quaker leanings. In his later years, Stephen's spirit may have begun to be troubled by his slave-owning. It is Stephen Hussey who is credited with building the meetinghouse of the Friends Society in Nantucket. The ancient Hebrew mystics had a phrase for such a good deed. It was *tikkun olam*—the work of repairing and healing the world. Stephen is buried there in the Friend's Burying Ground, next to the meeting house, but to this day, Shirk's resting place in Hampton, remains unmarked and unknown.

Negro Jack

There is almost nothing known about Negro Jack except that in 1689 he was accused of killing Isabel Holdred (Holdredge) in the Mast Swamp where the townships of Hampton, Exeter, and Stratham came together.[7] William Holdred, a tanner, and his wife, Isabel, likely met in Salisbury, Massachusetts, where they married in 1639. In 1667 they settled in Exeter, but not happily so for in 1676, William was bringing suit against Richard Scammon for failing to give him a firm deed on thirty acres of land he had purchased near Wheeler's Creek. Isabel had been a principal witness in a case against John Godfrey in 1659, while they lived in Massachusetts. Godfrey was accused of witchcraft, based in part on Isabel's emotional testimony against Godfrey. It had not been the only time that Isabel had seen strange things that left her shaken and disturbed.

Isabel was a widow when Negro Jack allegedly killed her. Although there seems to be no record of Negro Jack's trial, there is a record of his month-long imprisonment and his hanging in Boston on May 8, 1690.[8] The information that remains about Negro Jack is so meager that we are not able to know whether he was a free or owned man, his age, whether he had kin, or even whether he resided in Hampton. His deed occurred at the geographical margins of Hampton and his life story at the very edges of Hampton's history.

Unnamed black teenager (Langdon/Pottle)

The purchase of the third seventeenth-century slave of which we have notes, appears in the Langdon family papers:

> On June 16, 1699, Capt. Tobias Langdon of Portsmouth bought from Christopher Pottle, in Hampton, an unnamed black youth about sixteen or seventeen years of age (purchased for 30 pounds).[9]

(Also listed is this transaction, on September 10, 1718, Captain Tobias Langdon bought a "Negro Slave Named Hannah" for £36 from a J. Wentworth, not of Hampton.)

Christopher Pottle was a tanner who was baptized in 1704/5 in the First Congregational Church and admitted to full Communion in 1707. He was married to Hannah and several of his children were also baptized, including Hannah, Elizabeth, Sarah, and William. Christopher, however, was not connected with the church when the purchase of this teenager took place.

For what reason might a tanner have needed an "unnamed black youth" to help in the processing of leather, especially when he had several children of his own? To answer this question is to imagine a hard life for both tanner and slave. In the late 1600s, livestock such as goats, cows, or pigs were often slaughtered in the fall if there was not significant feed for them during the winter. The skin was then cleaned near running water and placed in great vats with lime and other organic material such as urine, fermenting rye, and dung in order to remove the animal hair. Later, more lime was used and then oak bark was added to achieve the brown coloring. After the hide was colored, a long soaking process came next. Toxic materials were added that burned the tanner's skin and left even the air around the tannery hard to breathe for the stench. It would be interesting to know if the unnamed black youth sold by Christopher Pottle was eager to exchange his tanning duties for those associated with Captain Langdon's trade—that of a wheelwright. Did Hannah, purchased nearly twenty years later, and the unnamed black youth come to know one another? Or did she and the unnamed black youth simply share the same Langdon slave cemetery plot in back of Christ Episcopal Church parsonage on Lafayette Road in Portsmouth, New Hampshire? We may not know since most of the headstones marking these slave graves are small and without inscription.

More than thirty years after Christopher Pottle sold his black youth to Capt. Tobias Langdon, Rev. Ward Cotton, seventh pastor of First Congregational Church of Hampton, came to lead the parish. He began his ministry in 1734, following a brief season of guest ministers who succeeded Rev. Nathaniel Gookin, whose journal ends in August of 1731. Rev. Cotton served the church faithfully for thirty-one years. His journal is the first to record the names (given to them by their owners) of several African Americans as well as Native Americans and even persons of Irish and Scottish descent. Their names were recorded as part of the on-going life of First Congregational Church. The persons, introduced below,

Langdon Family Burial Plot, Portsmouth, NH; possible burial site of the unnamed black youth owned by Christopher Pottle

enjoyed the sacraments of baptism and Communion. They "owned the covenant" and were taken into membership. Often, upon their deaths, a short testimony as to character was given by the pastor. Shirk walks across the page in the history of Hampton as a lone person as does Negro Jack and Christopher Pottle's unnamed black youth. But the slaves mentioned next are those whose presence within the church made for a truly diverse and beloved community.

CHAPTER 4

The Stories of African Americans, Both Slave and Free, in the Early Life of First Congregational Church

RECORD BOOK I AND II, as it is called, contains fragmentary records of Rev. Seaborn Cotton as copied by Rev. John Cotton, records of John Cotton's tenure as pastor, 1696–1710; records of Rev. Nathaniel Gookin's tenure, 1710–1734, and a portion of Rev. Ward Cotton's records, 1734–1766. There are no names of slaves recorded in either Rev. Seaborn Cotton's notes or Rev. John Cotton's notes. The record of slave names begins in Rev. Nathaniel Gookin's tenure and peaks during the pastorate of Rev. Ward Cotton.

Rev. Ward Cotton began as an assistant to Rev. Nathaniel Gookin just months prior to Rev. Gookin's death, following which Ward Cotton was ordained. It is fascinating to imagine that churches in Newton and Salisbury, Massachusetts; Providence, Rhode Island; and area New Hampshire churches such as those in Portsmouth, Exeter, Hampton Falls, Greenland, and Stratham sent representatives to Rev. Cotton's ordination. Present-day county boundaries are observed on such occasions and it would be rare today for any out-of-state representatives to be present at an ordination unless they were members of the pastor's previous church. Rev. Ward Cotton's ordination is also notable for having the first sermon preached by someone other than the candidate for ordination himself. In this case, Ward's brother, Rev. John Cotton of Newton, Massachusetts, preached the sermon.

At the time of his ordination there were 253 members in full Communion (84 women and 169 men). It wasn't more than three years into Cotton's ministry when it appears that the membership declined. In actual fact, a group of fourteen were dismissed under the leadership of Rev. Jeremiah Fogg, to form a new church in Kensington. Jeremiah had grown up in the Hampton church. Here he received his call to ministry and earned his seminary degree under the watchful eye of Rev. Cotton. In 1738, in Cotton's fourth year at Hampton, there is evidence from the annual meeting minutes of the church that the first mention of raising funds for "missionary" purposes appears. This was apportioned to "promote ye preaching of the Gospel in ye Towns of Providence, south Kingston and easterly within ye Colony of Rhode Island." The monies raised were delivered to Dr. Coleman and Dr. Sewall, men who were mentioned in chapter 1, for this purpose. The offering amounted to twenty pounds, the price of a healthy, Negro male slave. And where was this money going? It would end up in the New England colony with the largest population of slaves—Rhode Island. What mission were Coleman and Sewall excited about but the mission to end slavery.[1]

It is difficult to tell from extant records whether the increase in the number of slaves owning the covenant, becoming baptized, and attending church activities was due to the personality or length of tenure of Rev. Ward Cotton, who served faithfully for thirty-one years, or to the increase in evangelizing in which he and other area clergy were engaged. This increase may as easily have had to do with the general increase in the number of slaves in town, the growth of trades and industries, and their need of slaves' labor. One thing that is certain is that among all the names of African Americans listed, there is not one who ever was named a deacon, a role that was reserved for older, white males who were prominent not only by virtue of their wisdom and faith, but also because of their prominence in politics and trade. On the ancient records of pew owners, there is also not a single slave's name that appears, indicating that the social status of pew ownership was granted primarily to those who were successful and influential businessmen.

The early decades of the 1700s was a time of several "dismissals" of groups of church members from the First Congregational Church who formed "daughter" churches nearby. As happened in Hampton, usually the town and church shared closely both civic and religious histories. So as towns broke off from Hampton and were incorporated as distinct towns, so too, did the churches become separate from First Congregational Church of Hampton. These daughter churches included Hampton Falls (a small group dismissed in 1712, finalized in 1718), North Hampton (dismissed in 1719, finalized in 1742) and Kingston (petitioned for dismissal in 1694 and nine dismissed in 1725). From Hampton Falls, other dismissals created "granddaughter" churches in Kensington (1734) and Seabrook (1768). From Kingston, dismissals created churches in Sandown (1756), Danville (1735–1739, finalized in 1760), and East Kingston (1738). These eight parishes paralleled the growth in settlements north and west of Hampton. Since it was much easier for church women who carried food, foot warmers, and children with them to worship close to home, it meant that most of these dismissals were about six miles away from First Congregational Church in any direction.

Many of the named slaves in the Daughter and Grand-daughter parts of this document resided first in Hampton with

founding families who later took up residence in nearby towns
as new Congregational churches were incorporated. There,
they continued to marry, join as members, have their children
baptized, and enjoy the privilege of receiving the Sacrament of
Communion alongside the family who owned them. Although
the owners' names may have been mentioned in early records at
Hampton, their descendants and most of their slaves listed in
the second section of this document are not in the record books
of First Congregational Church but are listed in the record
books of the subsequent Congregational faith communities.

Cromwell

"Cromwell, a Negro man,"[2] [baptized and admitted to full
communion, November 5, 1727].

With nothing to go on beyond this one line in Rev.
Nathaniel Gookin's journal, it is difficult to say anything with
certainty about Cromwell—not his age, nothing about his
talents or vocation, nor his owner's name—or if he even had
an owner. Cromwell is simply this Negro man's name. We can
assert with some certainty that Cromwell was not a free man
since the majority of records of blacks from the early eighteenth
century who have a single name are slaves.

At times, it is impossible to find a context for a life, but
with each person named in the church journals, the process
of trying to discover an identity often begins with very little.
Although nothing is known for sure beyond what is listed above
for Cromwell, the process of discovery usually begins with spec-
ulation about an owner. An example of the investigative process
might look like this:

A Thomas Cromwell, born in Newbury, Massachusetts, moved to Hampton in 1639. In a family profile entitled
"Captain Thomas Cromwell, 17thC Pirate,"[3] Thomas Jones adds
that Thomas Cromwell participated in at least one voyage to the

West Indies in the 1630s. Later, in 1642, he sailed with Captain Jackson and wandered along the coast of South America, even invading the island of Margarita. It is believed that they sailed at least twice between South America and Jamaica over the next three years before returning to England. He then sailed back to Boston where he died accidentally in 1649. It is possible that on one of these trips, he brought back with him to Hampton certain slaves, since many of Hampton's early slaves were part of the triangle trade between England, the West Indies, and New England. But his death seems too early to have reasonably implied an ownership of this man, Cromwell, who was baptized at Hampton in 1727. Without a record that Cromwell is owned by Thomas Cromwell, we can move on to look elsewhere for an owner whose name may not be Cromwell.

The name Cromwell was given to an African-American man, whose life is linked with that of the Sherburne family of Hampton and Portsmouth. Captain Samuel Sherburne (b. 1638) came from Portsmouth to Hampton to manage the ordinary that had belonged to Robert Tuck and his relatives after Tuck's death. While living at Strawbery Banke in Portsmouth, the Sherburne family owned slaves, one of whom was Cromwell. We might wonder if Cromwell was brought to Hampton by Samuel and his wife, Love Hutchin(g)s to help with the upkeep of the ordinary. However, Samuel owned the ordinary from 1678 until he was killed in 1691. His widow, Love Hutchin(g)s, resided in Hampton for a time before moving to Kingston. She had joined the First Congregational Church, and one wonders if she may have inspired Cromwell to join the church prior to her death in 1739.[4] It is an interesting situation which seems relatively plausible.

The above scenario becomes impossible, however, if the runaway slave ad placed by Henry Sherburne Jr. on October 3, 1754, in both the *Boston Evening Post* and the *Boston Gazette* is describing the same Cromwell as mentioned above.[5] Why? Because although Henry Sherburne Jr. is Samuel Sherburne's great-grandson, he describes the runaway slave, Cromwell, as being forty-five years of age in this ad. This means Cromwell would not have been born when Samuel and Love arrived in Hampton to manage the Tuck Ordinary. His birth would have been about 1709, nearly the same age as Henry Jr.

What is actually more likely than these two scenarios is that Cromwell was a free man, since the listing of his baptism does not indicate that he was the slave or servant of anyone. If this is the case, it is a truly remarkable accounting, since very few African Americans were joining Puritan communities as free men or women prior to the mid-1700s. Sometimes exactly what is in the record is the most surprising truth of all!

Although we have little to go on as to whom Cromwell was, we may be able to gain a better idea of why he would want to be baptized and join the church. At the end of October 1727, Hampton experienced a forceful earthquake. The shaking from this earthquake, which occurred late in the evening on October 29, was attended with a terrible, thundering noise. Houses trembled and chimneys cracked and broke into pieces. Some persons recorded seeing a flash of light, perhaps lightening, and then streams of light running upon the earth giving off a bluish color. The sea roared and for several weeks afterward, after-shocks were experienced. With pastors in the pulpits encouraging their members to "hold fast in the Lord," perhaps Cromwell decided to do just that and owned the covenant—publicly confessing his sins, and placing his faith in God, his trust in Christ's leading, and his reliance on the Holy Spirit for his pilgrimage of faith. There are many reasons that a person might join a church. Fear for one's life or the securing of a home for your soul in God is perhaps one reason that could top anyone's list when lightning is running through the streets.[6]

Unnamed Negroes (Freese)

"A negro man aged 30 of Mrs. Freese's, died [January 13, 1736]."[7]

"Negro Woman of Mrs. Freezes aged 30: [died of] Throat ail: [January 15, 1736]."

"Negro Girl, her Dauter, aged 6: [died of] Throat ail: [January 16, 1736]."[8]

An unnamed Negro woman gave birth to a daughter when she was twenty-four years of age. There is no record that this child was ever baptized and no record that her mother was ever a member of First Congregational Church. Each appears in the record only as their lives end in what is likely a bout with the "throat distemper." This disease had started in Kingston in early 1735 and by autumn of that year cases were being recorded in Hampton. Many cases were like this where parent and child died within days of one another. The church record does not include the death of Mrs. Freese's Negro man. However, in Mr. Page's journal of epidemic deaths, he states that Mrs. Freese also had a male Negro servant who was thirty years of age who also died of the throat distemper in 1735/36. Could it be that this was a slave family?

Since this Negro woman lived with Mrs. Rachel Chase Freese, wife of Lt. Jacob Freese, it is likely that her work as well as her daughter's and the unnamed male servant's would have been related to tavern-keeping. Jacob Freese was a man of some means, but Rachel also inherited a goodly sum when her father, Joseph Chase, died in 1718. The tavern-keeping was therefore not Rachel's sole means of support. However, since Jacob died not long after the earthquake of 1727, he was not alive during the week between January 6 and January 15, 1736. Would Rachel have tried to tend her Negro servants while keeping the tavern open on behalf of grieving townsfolk and friends alike who were also losing family members or slaves as Rachel was?

One wonders how she could have done this since she lost her daughter, also named Rachel, during this same week to throat distemper. How did families survive such losses? For the most part, it seems they just went forward, for a year later, Rachel married her second husband, Col. Andrew Wiggin. He had grown up on his family farm, set off in Hampton until 1692, and then partitioned to Stratham. Although Mrs. Freese is named as owner of the Negro woman and her daughter as well as of the Negro man, all of whom died with the throat distemper; when her second husband, Andrew, died before her she did not inherit his slaves. Rather, upon Andrew Wiggin's death in 1753, he bequeathed to his grandson, Jonathan Wiggin, "half my saw mill and half greesmill and half my stock of cattel of all sorts half my wering close one cane one gun and my negro boy Loesses second child all him his heirs and assigns forever if he live to full age." Andrew also bequeathed to his grandson, Andrew Wiggin, the other half of the mills, cattle and clothing as well as, "my negro man Filander, him his heirs and assigns forever if he live to the age of 21."[7] It is left to the work of another to trace any church records in Stratham wherein Loesses second child or Filander may appear.

Caesar (Godfrey)

"Cesar, ye Negro of Widow Godfrey"[8] [baptized March 28, 1736].

Other than this record of his baptism, we know little about Caesar until the death of his master, Jonathan Godfrey. When Jonathan died March 13, 1734, he left a will. On p. 503 of *New Hampshire Wills*, vol. 3, is this sentence: "I also give and dispose of my Negro man, Caesar to my beloved wife, Mehitable to dispose of him as she pleaseth."[9]

Jonathan Godfrey had married Mehitable Blake (daughter of John Blake) in 1719 and became a member of First

Congregational Church in 1727. Mehitable had already been baptized in 1701. Ward Cotton's records indicate that these children were baptized in the church as well: Sarah, Hannah, Abigail, Mehitable, Isaac, and Elizabeth. It is not known whether Caesar was owned by Jonathan as early as 1719, the time of his marriage, and through the early years of Mehitable's child-bearing. After Jonathan's death, Mehitable married second husband Enoch Sanborn on April 1, 1736. It is interesting that Caesar's baptism occurred just three days before Widow Godfrey's marriage to Mr. Sanborn. Perhaps it was important to Mr. Sanborn that if he were going to own Caesar, that Caesar come already identified as a baptized Christian. After April 1, 1736, this Caesar, belonging to Widow Godfrey becomes the "Caesar, Negro servant of Enoch Sanborn," who is listed below.

Caesar, "a negro of Enoch Sanborn's – The first of that color that ever belonged to this Church" [admitted to full Communion, May 24, 1741].[10] This hand-written comment by Ward Cotton might have been added as a way to indicate the owner's pride in the Christian shepherding of his slave since the head of a Puritan family was obligated to educate both his children and his slaves in the stories of the faith. Enoch Sanborn's son, Isaac, was baptized in First Congregational Church in 1737, so within the first five years of his marriage to Mehitable, both his son and slave had participated in the two rites of the church—baptism and Communion. Enoch Sanborn died in 1762 and we might wonder if, upon his death, Caesar became a free, black man. There is no record of Caesar being manumitted by Enoch, but there is a record of a Caesar Godfrey who served his country.

In June 1793, in Nantucket, Massachusetts, there is a marriage recorded for a Caesar Godfrey and a Phebe Boston.[11] In 1800, the U.S. census shows two "free others" named Godfrey living in Nantucket. There is also listed Caesar Godfrey, a free black man, who declares in a pension application written in 1818, that in the War of the Revolution and at the time that Captain John Barry first took command of the Continental Frigate *Alliance*, he joined the navy to serve as a waiter and mariner. He does not remember the month and year of his joining but he was fifty-six at the time of declaration and he stated that when he joined he was "then but a boy." He was aboard during an engagement between the frigate *Alliance* and the British sloops of war *Atalanta* and *Trepassey* off the coast of Nova Scotia. Caesar suffered the loss of an eye during fighting. Caesar received about $135 dollars for his nine months of service.[12] It is quite likely that this mariner, Caesar Godfrey, was the son of the slave owned by Jonathan Godfrey and Enoch Sanborn. Since Caesar, the slave, is listed in 1734 as Jonathan Godfrey's "Negro man" he would have been older than twenty-one years of age to have been considered a man. Thus, the Caesar who applied for a pension in 1818, would have had to have been a younger Caesar. He would have been born in 1762—the year of Enoch Sanborn's death and perhaps also the year of the elder Caesar's freedom. Caesar and Phebe also are believed to have had a son named, Charles, who is buried in the Negro cemetery in Nantucket, Massachusetts.

Prince (Griffith)

"Prince, Negro Boy of Mr. Griffith's, aged 10 [died of] consumption"[13] [February 4, 1738].

Prince, like several other African Americans listed in Rev. Ward Cotton's journal, appears only at the time of his death. We know little else about this young man, and because of his early death by consumption, he did not live long enough to serve in the military, marry, or even gain his freedom, which might have given us a bit more information about what life was like for him. The little we know of Mr. Gershom Griffith, Prince's owner, is that he was born in 1707 and came to Hampton from

Portsmouth. He was a tavern keeper and trader, son of Dr. Caleb Griffith, a physician of Portsmouth. Although there is no record that he ever joined the First Congregational Church, it appears that his wife, Mary, joined in 1736. Several of his children were baptized in the church including William Sheafe, Nathan Sheafe, Olive, Ann, Abigail, Caleb, Elizabeth, and Sarah, who was baptized by Rev. Whipple of Hampton Falls. John Griffith Jr., another Griffith from Portsmouth, was also a shopkeeper and mariner. Whether John and Gershom were cousins is not known, but John married into the Lang family and when he died in 1777, his probated will records a payment to a Negro, Cato, for his share of prize money and a credit for "Cato, run off."[14]

Alice Page

"Allice Page, young woman of color," [was baptized on July 13, 1817. On that same day, she owned the covenant as well].[15]

Alice Page appears several times in various Hampton records and never once does she appear to have belonged to anyone but herself. She enters the record book in 1817 and just nine years later, on September 20, 1826, Alice dies in the night, alone. The Hampton Congregational Church record of her death says, "Alice Page, colored woman aged 27. Died in the night alone. Retired as usual. Had been unwell for most of the summer, but kept about and performed labor even the night of her death. She was found a corpse in the morning. Was an exemplary professor and had made, as we trust, considerable advance in a divine life."[16]

A second source corroborates this account with a similar one: "Sept. 20, 1826 Alice Page died at Mrs. Toppan's [Mrs. Edmund or Mary] suddenly appearing to drop away in sleep. She had been previously sick more than a year, not able to work for several months. Mrs. Toppan had brought her up from a child and she lived 20 years."[17]

Mrs Sarah Toppan agreed to pay said S Godfry
the Value of her work in clothing — April 1st 1820

Simon Godfry lost time 1820

August 23	1/2 day funeral James Lampry's child	25
28	To 1/2 day attending funeral Mrs C. Lampry	24
9	✻ attended funeral Child Simon Lampry	25
Sept 26	funeral Wiliam Browns child	25
	Mr More's child — Sept 29	25
29	Dr Lawrences child Sept 1 day	25
Nov 10	absent 1 day 13 1/2 day 14 1/2 day attending	$1 50
	funeral Mrs Towle —	
Dec 25	To 1/2 day funeral Mrs Blake Widow above	50
		50
	To 3 days lost time previous to this date	1 50
1821	Mary & June tolling bell & sweeping	1 50
Jany 7	To one day lost time at dear James funeral	50
	To 2 days lost time digging grave Mrs Perkins saturday	50
24	Simon Godfry 1 day absent funeral	50
Feb	To one day lost time	50
23	March 5 To 1 day digging Grave Anna Towle	50
	March 12th 1/2 dy lost time do 17 1/2 dy lost time	$1
1822	June 14th attending funeral Mrs J Mace digging G	$1
	June 15th attending funeral John Batchilder 1 day	
25	To topping pair shoes —	
July 19	To 1 day attending funeral Jethro Blake	$1
1823		

1826 Sept 26th Alice Page died at Mrs Toppan's
    sudenly appearing to drop away in
    sleep she had been previously sick more than
a year, not able to work for several months
Mrs Toppan had brought up from a child & she lived 20 yea

A third account of her death appears (with an error, I believe) in the North Hampton Congregational Church burial record. It states that September 23, 1826, "Alice Scott [Page] died at Esquire Toppan's at Hampton. Buried in this town a woman of colour, a reputable member of church in Hampton, sudden, age 27."[18] This should read Alice Page—the listing, Alice Scott, I believe is in error as an Alice Long from North Hampton was married to a William Scott. Alice Page did not marry.

Finally, a fourth account of Alice's death appears. The statement reads: "Alis Page, negro, who died September 20, [1826.]"[19] It is uncertain who the compiler of the Hampton List of Deaths is, but some sources suggest Edmund Toppan. It is highly unusual to have four separate accounts of the death of even the most high-born Caucasian, but even more unusual to have four records survive of the death of a mulatto child from two different town/church records. Alice must have been a reputable and well-appreciated woman.

Alice's mother is listed as Lucy Page (born 1772), daughter of Francis Page (born 1724) and Mary Marston. There is no mention of who Alice's father was. If Alice was listed as a "woman of color," then Alice's father was African American. One can only imagine what it might have been like for Lucy to discover her pregnancy, deliver her child, and then to be separated from that child, destined to live apart from her in a different home. Neither is it easy for one to imagine what it must have been like for Alice to have been separated from her mother at an early age! The record states that Alice Page lived

Left: Sarah Toppan's Account Book, A record of Alice Page's Death, Courtesy of the Hampton Historical Society Archives

for a number of years at Edmund Toppan's home. Although Edmund had practiced as a lawyer in both Portsmouth and Deerfield, New Hampshire, he did not think he truly fit in either place and had come back to Hampton in 1803, so Alice could have been a year or so, or merely months old when she was taken into the Toppan household. Edmund was married to Mary Chase (daughter of Stephen of Portsmouth) and there were six Toppan children in the house in which Alice grew up. Christopher Stephen, first child of Edmund, would have been born about the same year as Alice.

There are many instances in Rev. Ward Cotton's journal where a couple was made to confess that they had engaged in sexual activity prior to marriage. This was routinely required when an infant arrived at "seven months" rather than nine. The couple's dual confession needed to be given before the congregation and accepted as sincere and truthful prior to the child's birth, as baptism might be denied without confession. The early Puritans believed that a child who was not baptized was a soul denied the opportunity for everlasting life. So parents often suffered the public humiliation of a verbal confession for the sake of their child's soul. At times, a fine was levied or written confessions were required and read publicly. All of this was required from Caucasian couples who intended to marry anyway. It was far more severe for a white woman to have engaged in sexual activity with an African American, especially if he was a slave. Lucy Page may have incurred not only ecclesiastical shunning but public consequences as well.

Town officials were loath to imagine bearing the burden of care for an illegitimate, mulatto child who would necessarily become a ward of the town. Juliet Haines Mofford, in her work *The Devil Made Me Do It!* tells the story of Maybell Evance, who in 1719 went before the Essex County Court for bearing an illegitimate child. She accused a black slave named Gregory, who belonged to Francis Norwood of Lynn, Massachusetts. Maybell was whipped "15 stripes and costs" and was "to serve the selectmen of Beverly and their assigns, five years toward the town's maintenance of her child." Oddly enough, Gregory challenged the truth of Maybell's assertion, claiming that he was not guilty of fathering her child. He offered, however, to take on the care of the child and Maybell asserted that she, then, wished to marry him. Ultimately Gregory was the one who was punished. He received twenty lashes, was sold out of the province within six months, and jailed in the meantime.[20] It stretches the limits of good reason to punish and export the willing supporter of a black child who was possibly not his own, when by doing so the town would have been relieved of the burden they feared. Perhaps within this detail lies the devil who made them do it!

The Hampton church record is silent on the consequences of Lucy Page's birth of Alice, "her child of colour," except for the obvious fact that Alice was fostered out to the Toppan family and Lucy moved to North Hampton. There is also no reference to consequences to a father, since no father is listed.

With regard to illegitimate births, the midwives also played significant roles in Puritan communities. This was due to the belief that at the peak of labor, if nagged by the midwife, the laboring mother could not help but reveal the name of the father. If this happened, it meant that the midwife was often called as a witness so the town would know to whom they could go for child support. If a single woman gave birth and refused to name the father, it occasionally happened that the woman was accused of prostitution, a much more serious crime. Since there is also no record of such an accusation against Lucy Page, it seems that the town may have been content to require only the early adoption of Alice into the Toppan home, where they would be assured that the child would not become a drain on the public coffers.

Since mulatto children followed the mother's "condition," if a white woman were to give birth to a child of colour, that child would have been considered free. Since this fact meant an increase in the population of free blacks, such an event would have been kept as quiet as possible. If the father was known, he was fined and sometimes whipped. Regardless of how Lucy became pregnant with Alice, it appears that both Lucy and Alice lived unmarried lives—one in North Hampton, the other in Hampton.

By 1801, Lucy would have lost two brothers—her brother Daniel to drowning and her brother Coffin in 1801. Alice, born about the same time as Coffin died, was given away. Then, just a year later, both Lucy's mother and father died in North Hampton (in 1802); Mary of fever and Francis of urinary obstructions. It is safe to assume that both of them would have needed tending prior to their deaths.

One wonders how Lucy would have coped with the loss of nearly all her close family. Was she ever able to travel to Hampton to visit Alice—perhaps in those years after her parents' deaths? Did Alice get to know her mother or did the Toppans in an attempt to protect everyone involved from further scandal, keep Alice from knowing her birth mother?

Twenty years passed and then in 1822, John Page, Lucy's brother, died. Did Lucy believe the specter of death had returned to strike again multiple times? Well she might have, for both Lucy and Alice died within four years of John's death. The record is silent on whether there was ever a reunion between Alice and Lucy. But the record is clear on another aspect of Lucy's story and is offered in phrases from the North Hampton Vital Records. In 1826, pauper burial services were provided for Lucy Page. Next to the date of Lucy's burial—"Lucy Page, buried June 15, 1826, at age 52"—are these words, "died of intemperance [alcoholism] and dropsy."[21]

It seems that Lucy endured both loneliness and illness without the comfort of her only child to care for her. Alice, at least, had the kind regard of the Toppan family and the church family as certain comforts at the end of her life. Just as Robert Page was a well-loved deacon for many years in the church, dying about one hundred years before Alice Page's own death. So too, Alice is remembered as one who had made considerable advance in her divine life—becoming an "exemplary professor" of scripture by the time of her death. These words of Rev. Josiah Webster, "exemplary professor," are truly amazing in retrospect. Josiah Webster was a man deeply concerned about the value and necessity of learning and persevered for more than a decade toward deepening the spiritual life of his flock with little sign of an increase in either faithfulness or numbers. So, he turned his energy toward founding the Hampton Academy as a center of learning first for men and later including women. Rev. Webster was instrumental in founding the church school program by 1818 within the church, but it was not until 1827 that suddenly he received more than fifty new members and saw the fruits of his labors in a new-born spirit alive in his congregation. Everywhere he turned, Rev. Webster tried to cultivate "professors," and when he thinks about Alice Page's life he says, "exemplary, undoubtedly more worthy than many." Did he include the white members of his congregation when he spoke thus? If we say, yes, we may also conclude that here, Alice's pastor was looking beyond her color, beyond her life circumstances to see in her heart and soul that zest for knowledge and that divine yearning that he wished for all his beloved community. Her foster family and her faith family may have opened the door for Alice to these treasures that Rev. Webster acknowledges, but she walked through it.

CHAPTER 5

Slaves Owned by Physicians, from the Church Record Book

T HE BELOW-MENTIONED SLAVES, FLORA, Jock and Simon, all served in the homes of physicians of Hampton. In the early days of the Hampton settlement, physicians were often referred to as "chirugeons" or surgeons. Those so trained could perform surgical procedures as well as pull teeth, set broken limbs, perform bleedings and concoct simple preparations that would induce vomiting or purging. A physician was expected to lay more stress on the natural, moral, and physical aspects of a man and to display a temperate "complexion." Another expectation was to be a "good liver and keeper of the holy commandments of God."[1] This may have been the euphemistic way of saying that the physician should not let strong drink cause his hands to quake nor have a "wandering eye" that would lead to "spouse-breaking." Above all, the physician should be learned, imaginative, and well-mannered with his patients. It would seem that such a temperate complexion might have the advantage of offering any young slave or servant living under the same roof a great father-figure or preceptor.

By the time of the Revolutionary War, thirty-five hundred practicing physicians joined the regiments across the colonies to provide care for soldiers and sailors. Of these, perhaps only three hundred had been to medical school, where their primary course would have been Latin.

Robert Tuck, a noted "chirugeon," emigrated from Suffolk, England, to Hampton. He was among the first settlers of Hampton. At the time in history when Robert Tuck's practice began, most physicians had only an undergraduate degree and learned their trade by apprenticing with barbers or butchers. In order to be a "doctor's boy" or servant in a chirugeon's home, important requirements may have included the ability to stand the sight of blood, a willingness to run to the apothecary, a willingness to ride horseback with messages and the same even temper that was required at the bedside of the ill.

Despite the character building or learning of the physician's trade that was possible, if African American "doctors' boys," themselves, fell ill, the doctor who owned them was under no compunction to heal them with the same array of medicinal aids as administered to white persons who fell ill. Once a slave grew weak or no longer useful it was sometimes the case that he or she would be given over to other slaves who knew the youth so he would receive some care. Since slaves had no purchasing power for medicines, they frequently resorted to herbal remedies. But it was hard work, a poor diet, and the reality of fewer hours of rest that wore down the immune systems of servants and slaves so their ability to fight illnesses was lessened. So it was that children, both blacks and whites, were easy prey for the "throat distemper" epidemic that started in Kingston and hit Hampton beginning about 1735.

The throat distemper or diphtheria epidemic proved the most strenuous time of service for physicians and therefore for their servants. Blood-letting was the usual procedure when the hallmark symptoms of a swollen, white-flecked throat, profound weakness, and the appearance of the tough slime that ultimately suffocated patients first appeared. Sometimes, in this particular disease, the blood-letting was done under the tongue, with a honey-vinegar liquid that included dissolved alum used as a gargle after the procedure. During the time of the throat distemper in Hampton, dozens of persons died and the records indicate whole families that were lost to the disease. Several of the African American servants or slaves, whose stories follow, were affected by the throat distemper epidemic.

Simon (Jackson?)

"Simon, ye Negro boy of Doctor [Clement] Jackson" [baptized April 23, 1738][2]

Other than knowing that Simon was baptized in 1738, there is a little more that gives us a view into his life. In 1742, Rev. Ward Cotton established the Second Society of Young Men as a means to encourage the moral life of young males. One of the signatures to this document is that of "Simon Jackson." None of Dr. Clement Jackson's children is named Simon, so it is likely that this Simon was Dr. Jackson's Negro boy. Since Simon belonged to Dr. Jackson, who served the town of Hampton as a physician between 1731 and 1747, it is likely that Simon knew "Flora, a Negro girl," listed below as belonging in Dr. Toppan's family along with the Negro boy of Mrs. Toppan. Simon may have even known Jock, Dr. Sargent's Negro servant. Simon, Flora, and Jock may have found a small measure of friendship as they hunted for herbs, passed one another on the streets carrying messages between doctor and patient, or sharing balcony pews in the meetinghouse.

Flora (Toppan)

"Flora, A Negro Girl of ye Widow Toppans"[3] [baptized June 7, 1741] and "A Negro Boy of Mrs. Toppans," [died March 11, 1740], aged 2 years of "fitts."[4]

In November 1739, at thirty-eight-years old, Dr. Edmund Toppan died of consumption. Not quite three months later, on February 9, 1740, Edmund, son of Widow Sarah Toppan, died at age one of "fitts." On March 11, Mrs. Toppan's negro boy aged 2 years, died of fitts. Death had become Sarah Toppan's constant, unwelcome companion. Then, a year later, Flora, Negro girl of Widow Toppan's was baptized. What a joy that sacramental moment must have been for Sarah, relieving the grief that had lingered long in the Toppan household. The record Rev. Cotton left does not give an age for Flora when she is baptized. But what if the Negro boy who died aged two years was Flora's brother or her son? Two women both suffering loss, perhaps both finding some measure of peace in the knowledge that important moments in their lives would be remembered, if nowhere else, than in the faith community's record. Baptized on this same day along with Flora was another set of women, "Margarett, ye daughter of Abigail Prince, an Indian woman" and "Jenny, A Negro girl of Ward and Joanna Cotton." (See section on clergy-owned slaves). Margarett, a child of yet another ethnic group, the local Native Americans of Hampton, also represents another of the untold stories of the early faith community.

Flora, Edmund and Sarah's Negro girl, was not however, the first Toppan family slave. Years earlier in 1637, Sarah Taylor Toppan and Abraham Toppan, ancestors of Edmund Toppan, had come to Newbury, Massachusetts, on the *Mary Ann* with a young child—their 3-year-old son, Peter. Peter had been born in 1633 in England and grew to become a physician in Newbury, while continuing his father's merchant trading business with Barbados. Peter owned sheep along with four other sheep owners in Newbury as well as one Negro servant, valued at thirty pounds sterling. Peter's servant was named Robert Jacklin, and he served Peter Toppan for twenty years. During this time,

Robert worked during his off hours to establish credit toward earning his freedom in a wage market. After Peter Toppan died from an untimely fall off Beniah Titcomb's wharf in 1707, his sons granted Robert Jacklin's freedom. Robert Jacklin traveled north to Londonderry, where he married a widow with three children. He and his family actually fared well because they owned land together.

Dr. Edmund Toppan was one of Peter's grandsons. He grew up in Newbury, Massachusetts, continued in the profession of his grandfather and became a physician, graduating from Harvard in 1720. In June of 1727 he married Sarah Wingate. In 1727, he moved to Hampton, where he practiced medicine until his death in November of 1739. Edmund is known to have sold to Edward Shaw, September 30, 1731, "Jack, an Indian man."[5] In the 1732 inventory of Hampton, Jack was valued at eighteen pounds.

There is no way to tell if Jack and Flora ever met before Jack was sold to Mr. Shaw, but I would like to imagine that Flora was the last African American to be owned by Edmund Toppan's family and that Flora was able to enjoy her freedom at some point. These two records indicate that earlier generations of the Toppan family owned slaves—both African American and American Indian in the years prior to the mention of Flora. The Toppans are not the first, nor will they be the last family in Hampton to have owned slaves for more than one generation.

Widow Toppan may have kept Flora in the family after Edmund's early death since she lived several decades longer than her husband. Or there is certainly a possibility that Flora, the Negro girl of Dr. Anthony Emery, mentioned below, could be the same Flora who belonged to Widow Toppan. Sarah Toppan may have noticed a talent in Flora for recognizing herbs or maintaining a calm presence at the bedside. If so, Flora would have been a great asset to Dr. Emery, who may have acquired her when he began his practice in Hampton. Flora, as it happens, is also the name given to a Negro servant whose presence is recorded in the Congregational Church records in South Hampton, New Hampshire. South Hampton was made up of pieces of both Salisbury and Amesbury, Massachusetts. In 1743, the first year of its incorporation as a town, a list of Negroes living in the town includes "Flora (Negro) servant of Mr. Ring's." Thereafter, several of Flora's children are listed as being baptized in the South Hampton Congregational Church, including: Lidia (1743), Flora (1745), Phillis (1747), Kate (1748), Fortune, son, (1749) and twins, Violet and Chloe (1755).[6] It is clearly conjecture as to whether Sarah Toppan might also have sold Flora to Mr. Ring after Edmund's death. They could, indeed, only be the same person if Flora was old enough to marry and give birth two years after her baptism.

Flora (Emery)

Dr. Anthony Emery owned "Flora, Negro Girl of Dr. Emerys aged 22 [died] of throat ailment" [on March 27, 1756.][7] We know very little about Flora except her date of death. It is possible that she is the same Negro girl of Widow Toppan's since Dr. Emery moved to Hampton in 1750, well after Widow Toppan's husband Edmund might have employed Flora in tasks related to his practice of medicine. Dr. Emery had graduated from Harvard Medical School in 1736, married Abigail Leavitt in 1738 and served for a time as physician in Chelmsford, MA. He bought Dr. Clement Jackson's place and soon began to build a reputation in Hampton as a man who led an active, useful and honorable life, with an extensive medical practice. While treating the folks of Hampton, Dr. Emery also carried on a trade with the West Indies. No other slaves were discovered in church or town records as belonging to Dr. Emery other than Flora.

Jock (Sargent)

"Jock, ye Negro Servant of Dr. Sargent"[8] [baptized July 5, 1741].
[owned the covenant July 5, 1741]

Jock, would have been baptized a month later than Flora
and three months before Fortunatas, Abner Fogg's Negro lad.
One wonders why so many African Americans, like Jock, were
baptized in the space of a few months in 1741.

It may have been due to any number of causes, but Rev.
George Whitefield was active in New England at this particular time. Rev. Whitefield was one of several traveling preachers
who helped to usher in the "Great Awakening," following in the
footsteps of Rev. Jonathan Edwards. Only twenty-five years old
when he burst upon the scene, George Whitefield whisked the
revival fire started by Edwards into white hot flames through
all of New England. When he preached, Whitefield, who was
only of average height, jumped about like a jack-in-the-box. His
eyes flashed and his powerful voice volleyed the truths of the
Gospel "like so many cannonballs" across the bow of a great
ship. When he spoke, hearts melted as he invited his listeners
to consider making a personal decision for Christ that would
change them from ordinary men and women into new beings.[9]
How could anyone resist, least of all those who truly wished to
be new beings who were free in Christ? Whitefield also encouraged a new worship style that was not based on intellect alone,
but which swelled with feeling and left congregants weeping,
deeply convinced of their need for change. How could this not
tap into the anguish of hearts that wanted such change, perhaps
more than we will ever know? Was Jock's life affected by such
sentiment? It seems many hearts were as the membership of First
Congregational swelled in 1742 by nearly one hundred people.

Dr. Nathaniel Sargent, owner of Jock, was a physician
in Hampton during this time. He was born in 1687, son of

Edward and married Dorothy Bradstreet. Nathaniel remained a physician in Hampton until about 1748 when he resettled in Portsmouth. In the 1732 Inventory of Hampton, there is listed this entry: "Dr. Sargent's negro slave, Jock....(value) 12 pounds." It seems likely from the record that Jock was owned first by Dr. Sargent and then given to his son, Dr. Sargent Jr., also a Hampton physician. Dorothy, Dr. Sargent's wife grew ill and died in 1743, aged fifty-one. Jock may have helped to care for her as she lay dying and his services would certainly have been needed by Dr. Sargent to keep up his medical practice and his home, after her death.

Dr. Sargent Jr. and his wife, Ruth, had three children: Edward, Joseph and Ruth. In the probated will of his father Nathaniel Sargent, Scipio, his Negro boy, is bequeathed to his unmarried daughters for five years, and then to his grandson, Edward. The reason Nathaniel does not bequeath anything to his son, Nathaniel Jr., is that he had died before his father.[10] As evidenced below, the daughters were only to receive Scipio if they were still unmarried at the time of the proving of the will:

> Moreover, If my Daughter Dearborn, & my youngest Daughter should see Cause (after my decease) to live together, or if they should live singly, in an unmarried Estate, Then I give unto them my said Daughters the Improvement of my Negro Boy Scipio, his Time equally divided between them, during the Space of five Years next insuing after my decease. They equally maintaining him in suitable Meat, Drink, Washing & Lodging during said Term of five Years. They shall have no Liberty to sell him, or send him out of the Country. And after the Expiration of the s*^ Term of Five Years, I give my said Negro Boy Scipio, (as Part of his Portion) to my

Grandson Edward Sargent, & his Mail Heirs during Life. If my said Daughters should both marry before the Expiration of s'^ five Years, then, upon the Day that the last of them shall marry, I give my said Boy, to my said Grandson.[11]

Since all of Nathaniel's daughters were married by 1767 when the five-year term was ended, this means that there is a chance that Scipio became "part of the portion" given to Nathaniel's grandson, Edward. Edward's father died one year before his grandfather died, so Edward could have inherited both Scipio and Jock, one slave from each of the previous generations.

CHAPTER 6

Other Hampton African Americans Who Established Families

Fortunatas (Fogg)

"Fortunatas, A negro Lad of Abner Fogg's" [who was baptized October 11, 1741] who "also owned the Covenant."[1]

Fortunatas's baptism and membership rites would have occurred just after Abner and Bethia Fogg gave birth to their daughter, Bethia. There is no indication of how old Fortunatas was when he was baptized, nor is there any indication of what he might have done for work as a lad in the Fogg family. Abner is listed as a yeoman and although several of his children were baptized in First Congregational Church, eventually Abner moved his family to North Hampton. We know that Abner moved his family by 1776, since his name is on the "Association Test" document for the town of North Hampton. This document was written by the New Hampshire Committee of Safety, under the chairmanship of Meshech Weare (later to become the first constitutional "president," or governor, of the state). The committee consisted of several leading legislators chosen to act when the legislative body was not in session. The document called for two actions: the signatures of every adult male willing to take arms against the British and the names of all those who refused to sign. We should note the exclusion, not only of "Lunaticks, Idiots, and Negroes," but also of women who were just as often not considered as full persons, and therefore not able to defend the colony against Britain.[2]

It is unlikely that Abner Fogg acquired Fortunatas from Rev. Joseph Whipple of Hampton Falls. For although in 1733, Rev. Whipple baptized a "Negro boy" named Fortunatas; in 1754, Rev. Joseph Whipple, pastor of the church of Hampton Falls, is quoted in his probated will as stating, "I give and bequeath to my servant man, Fortunatus [sic], his freedom from my service after the expiration of one and one-half years from March 23, 1754 provided he endemnifies [sic] my estate from all charge respecting him and also 5 pounds money old tenor to be paid to my Executrix, Elisabeth [Cutt Whipple]."[3] It is noted in Rev. Whipple's diary that he also purchased slaves named Pompey and Fortune, neither of which are part of the First Congregational Church of Hampton's Records.[4]

A Fortunatas Fogg enlisted in the Revolutionary War in May 1777 in the company of Capt. Isaac Warren in Col. John Bailey's 2nd Massachusetts Regiment. He served at Saratoga, spending a winter in Fort Ticonderoga and fighting at Monmouth. He was discharged in 1780 and is found in Exeter, New Hampshire.[5] In the 1790 census Fortunatas is listed along with a household of six other persons who were "free, non-white." In the Exeter records is listed a marriage between Fortune Fogg and Lucy Hale July 15, 1781. By 1800, the census lists a Fortune Fogg in Exeter with only three in the household and no further census includes this name. In the 1790 census for the town of Exeter, Scipio Fogg (head of family of two) is listed. Scipio may be a relative of Fortune's.[6] A William Daverson, living in Portsmouth in 1810, married an Ann-Marie Fogg who was designated as "colored."[7] Ann Marie may also have been a daughter of Fortunatas.

Abner Fogg had a brother, Jeremiah, who grew up in the Hampton Congregational Church. Jeremiah became an ordained minister. In 1734, Rev. Jeremiah Fogg married Elizabeth Parsons and traveled with her and her slave, Phillis, to begin his tenure as first pastor in Kensington, New Hampshire. Kensington is one of the "granddaughter" towns of Hampton, incorporated at a time when the "daughter" church of Hampton Falls dismissed members to form a parish in Kensington. (Phillis's story will appear as a later entry under Ebenezer Mingo.)

Lucy (Marston)

"Lucy, a Molatto Child presented by Obadiah Marston" [for baptism–September 22, 1754][8]

Obadiah Marston was born in 1710 and baptized that same year in the First Congregational Church. By 1754, when Lucy was baptized, Obadiah had become a shoemaker who lived at Little Boar's Head with his wife, Elizabeth Rawlins (Rollins) and their several children, all of whom were baptized at First Congregational Church. Since Obadiah's children had all been born by 1748, he would have been bringing this mulatto child, Lucy, for baptism when she was of a similar age to one of his grandchildren—perhaps close in age to his daughter Hannah's first child. The baptism record does not say that Lucy is Obadiah's child—merely that he presents her for baptism. Perhaps she is a granddaughter?

With only one name to go by, we know little of Lucy. Was she born in Obadiah's home? Since Elizabeth Rawlins grew up in a family who had owned slaves over several generations, Lucy may have come to live with the Marstons upon the death of one of Elizabeth's relatives' slaves. The record says little of Lucy's circumstances but this quote from Sarah Gudger, North Carolina ex-slave, gives one an idea of what a house servant might have been asked to do:

I never knowed what it was to rest. I just work
all de time from mornin' till late at night. I had to do
everythin' dey was to do on de outside. Work in de
field, chop wood, hoe corn... till sometimes I feel like
my back surely break... In de summer we had to work
outdoors, in de winter in de house. I had to card and
spin till ten o'clock. Never get much rest, had to get
up at four de next mornin' and start again.[9]

In 1779, by which time Lucy may have been freed, there is a
record of a Luci Marston being warned out of Seabrook.[10] If
this is the same Lucy Marston, she would be about twenty-five
years of age. Obadiah Marston was one of the last children born
in his family. About twenty years prior to his birth, in 1689, his
parents had given birth to a daughter who died within weeks.
Her name was Lucy, which means "light of God." There is no
Hampton record of the death of Lucy, "Mulatto child presented
for baptism." But if she was, indeed, named after Obadiah's
sister, Lucy, whom he never knew, perhaps it was because in this
mulatto child, God's light shone anew for Obadiah.

Caesar (Marston)

"Cesar, a negro man of Capt. Jeremiah Marston died ye 10 day
of April, 1766."[11]

"Caesar, a Negro man of Capt. Jeremiah Marston, died of
old age," [April 10, 1766].

There is not a list of duties that Caesar might have been
given by Capt. Marston, but it is fair to say that he probably
helped on the homestead, in the malt house, pruning fruit trees,
and cutting marsh hay in season. In the days just before the
French and Indian War, Captain Jeremiah set about to put his
things in order and wrote in his will: "I order my wife to: sell
my Negro and lay out ye money towards bringing up my son,
Simon to learning."[12]

Having written his wishes, he enlisted as a soldier in Capt. Sherburne's unit. This unit landed in Louisburg, Cape Breton, in February of 1745 and by May, Jeremiah had been killed fighting the French and Indians. This Negro whose sale was meant to provide Simon with his education was Caesar. Caesar must have been spared this sale out of the Marston family, however. Instead of being sold as property to provide for Simon's education, Caesar ended up as a slave in Simon's brother's family.

Simon Marston had, indeed, planned on obtaining a college education. He studied Latin and Greek, but due to poor health, he deferred more study and became a farmer, like his father, eventually moving with his family to Ossipee, New Hampshire, where he died in 1799. Before he moved, Simon must have turned the homestead over to his brother, Jeremiah Jr. It is likely that Caesar remained a slave at the family home-stead and it is interesting that in the record book, even unto his death, he is listed as Capt. Jeremiah's Negro man and not Jeremiah Jr's. Since Jeremiah Jr. had been deeded the cattle, horses, sheep, and swine, and had nine children with his wife, Tabitha Dearborn, there would have been a lot of work for Caesar to do. There he stayed, until he died, of old age, in 1766.

Cesar Long, A Free Negro

Cesar Long is listed in the Hampton Congregational Church records as being a free Negro, and this notation is the first of its kind in the record left us by Rev. Ward Cotton. Since it is clear that Cesar is free as of 1756, it means that at some point Cesar may not have been free. One question might be, to whom did Cesar belong and when did he become a free man? Such a ques-tion might seem to imply that slave ownership provides a clearer trail of information to the reader regarding Cesar's roots, or a better day-to-day context in which to place Cesar. Ironically, this is often true, in that records are left that indicate whether he was asked to work the fields, help with physicians' tasks or the duties of ship masters. If Cesar had tried to run away, an advertisement for his capture and return would have described his height and weight along with other physical attributes.

As a free African man, Cesar would have stood out in 1756, despite the fact that freedom, for whites or blacks in colonial Hampton, was crucial for success and the success of one's children and grandchildren. Many African American couples refused to have children of their own unless the mother was free, for the freedom of the mother determined the freedom of the children. When George Long, "son of Cesar a free Negro," is baptized in 1756, then Cesar's freedom would have meant that George, at birth, was still not considered free.

The *Boston Gazette* published numerous ads concerning "run-aways" and in May of 1733, this ad appeared in the newspaper:

> On the 18th instant Run-away from his Master Mr. Richard Long of Salisbury, A Negro Man, about 24 years of age, a lusty thick set Fellow, had on a brown homespun Coat & Waistcoat, and a new pair of Shoes. Whoever secures the said Negro, so that his said Master may have him again shall receive as a Reward Three Pounds, besides being paid all necessary Charges.[13]

There is no record linking Cesar to Richard Long of Salisbury, but such ads give a clue as to one way in which a slave might win his freedom—by simply running away!

In the First Congregational Church records there is not a wife listed for Cesar Long. However, in the North Hampton Church records there is a "Dinah, wife of Cesar Long," who died in 1774 [1779 in a second source] at age 55. If this is Cesar's wife, and they were about the same age, then Cesar and

Dinah would have been born between 1719 and 1724. Dinah seems also to be free. One North Hampton source states that Dinah died of intoxication. Perhaps Dinah's intoxication was the reason that Cesar and Dinah lived apart in two separate towns and why the children lived with Cesar and not Dinah.[14]

A Cesar Long served in the Revolutionary War from New Hampshire. In the records, his name was also spelled "Loney"[15] and his term of duty is not specific, except to know that it started on July 10, 1776, when he enlisted in Capt. Samuel Nay's company in Col. Joshua Wingate's regiment. Nay's company was ordered to "repair to Charles Town on the Connecticut River" before continuing on to join the army.[16]

Tales of litigation on Cesar Long's part over the course of several years are also recorded in Hampton's town records. In 1757 he appears as a plaintiff in action against the town of Hollis.[17] In 1758 he was a plaintiff in Hampton. He had been working for John Redman at the time of the small pox epidemic. While caring for the Redman family, the Hampton constable asked Cesar to also go to Dr. Emery's home to make a fire. Cesar responded by going to the Emery's two hours later and declared that he had so much to do, that he could not have gone earlier. When the epidemic was over, Cesar did not receive payment for his care of the Redman family and this caused him to sue the town for payment. Thirdly, he is mentioned in a New Hampshire Assembly petition from 1760 brought by Nathan Blake. Blake states that when he came home from the war after serving in Col. John Goffe's New Hampshire regiment under Capt. Jeremiah Marston, that he came down with smallpox. He says, "nobody was with me for some days but one Caezar Long." Cesar was not paid for this service either, so sued once more.[18] Finally, he is mentioned in 1761 in court action where this time he was the complainant. Walter Neal owed him forty pounds with interest of 15 percent. Neal lost the decision and appealed, but the complaint was upheld in 1762 in Cesar's favor.[19]

Certain researchers believe that Cesar came to Hampton from Chester or Raymond and may have been the slave of Benjamin or Joseph Long. It may have been possible for Cesar to have been the slave of their father, Nathan Long, but I believe that Benjamin and Joseph would have been born too late to have freed Cesar by 1756, if, indeed, he belonged to either Benjamin or Joseph.

Nathan Long (b. 1717) was from Newbury, Massachusetts. Nathan became a surveyor by 1747 and he settled on lot #99 in Chester. In 1748, he married Naomi Eastman. They had two children, Benjamin; born in 1750, who married Mary Colby; and Joseph, born in 1752, who married Mary's sister, Judith Colby. Benjamin eventually moved to New York State, and Joseph settled on the homestead in Chester. Both Benjamin and Joseph participated in the Revolutionary War according to "Old Chester" town records. There is no written connection as of yet, to indicate that any of the Chester, New Hampshire, Longs owned Cesar at any point.

Alice Long

"Alice, Negro child of Cesar Long, Baptized privately. It lived." [September 18, 1759];

"Alice, a Negro child of Cesar's N. Hill, aged one year – [Died] consumption from its birth"[20] [August 27, 1760];

"Alice, ye Daughter of Cesar Long, [baptized] by Brother"[21] [February 21, 1762];

"An Infant Child of Ceser Long's died ye 21 day of September," [1766].[22] Not either Alice, but an unnamed child.

In the First Congregational Church of Hampton records, Cesar is actually listed as having two daughters named Alice. His first daughter was baptized in 1759 and must have been at risk since it was noted that she was baptized privately. Private baptisms were usually administered if the family or pastor believed that the child was close to death. It is interesting to note that when Alice did not die, this fact was recorded by two words, "It lived," and not "she lived." There is a record that follows this entry, on August 27, 1760, that states, "Alice, a Negro child of Cesar's, North Hill aged one year, [died of] consumption." The second record of a baptism for an Alice, daughter of Cesar, occurs in 1762. This record states that Alice was baptized by Ward Cotton's brother. It must have been Rev. Josiah Cotton, as he was the only brother who lived long enough to have baptized Alice in 1762. A few years later, in 1766, the record indicates that an infant child of Cesar Long's dies. Because the church record does not include the child's name, it cannot be certain whether this child was a male or a female. It was probably not Alice, born 1762, but it does indicate that Cesar in Hampton must have had contact occasionally with Dinah in North Hampton, to have fathered another child.

In the records of the North Hampton Congregational Church, one of the daughter churches of Hampton, there is a record of a marriage between a William Scott (a man of color) and Eles (Alice) Long in 1791. Rev. Benjamin Thurston married them.[23] So, it seems, Alice Long, born 1762, did survive, and the infant child who died in 1766 was a different child of Cesar's, one who remains unnamed. Later, in a list of North Hampton deaths, a Pamela Scott (a black person) died of consumption in 1810—perhaps a daughter to Alice and William? William died suddenly in 1829 at the supposed age of eighty years, more than twenty years after Alice Scott, "a woman of color, wife of William Scott," had died of consumption in 1807.[24] Alice Scott's father, Cesar Long, had tended families in Hampton in 1758 who had small pox. Alice Long Scott's husband, William, would have tended a wife who died of consumption almost fifty years later.

George (Jorge) Long

"George [Jorge] ye, Son of Cesar, a Free Negro," [was baptized September 12, 1756].[25]

This is the only mention of Cesar Long's son George that is contained in the church record. George Long also is believed to have served in the Revolutionary War, but there is scant information about George in any other context save his baptism record. The North Hampton, New Hampshire, Revolutionary War rolls include the information that Jorge is named on a petition for wages due for service in the army. The petition was filed May 30, 1785.[26] George would have been about 29 years old, but no further record was found.

Paul (or Pasol or Peter) Long

Paul (or Pasol or Peter) Long is not listed in the Hampton Congregational Church records. But he shows up in the North Hampton Revolutionary Rolls and appears to have enlisted in 1777 in Captain Weare's Company for three years. Later, North Hampton Church records tell us that he married Phebe Swain of Newburyport, Massachusetts, in 1784. Phebe joined the church in 1789 and Paul and joined the North Hampton Congregational Church after his Revolutionary War service, in 1809.[27] It is likely that Paul is an older brother to George and Alice since his birth date is most likely in the year 1752; George was born in 1756 and Alice (who survived) was born in 1762. Various sources use the names Paul, Peter, and Pasol as interchangeable for the same person. However, there is still a possibility that Peter was yet another sibling in the Long family.

In 1769 there is a record of Merryfield Berry buying a Peter Long (slave) of Samuel Whidden (ran away after purchase). It follows, then, that this same Peter Long is one of three runaway slaves who were listed in an ad in the *New Hampshire Gazette*, dated November 2, 1775:

Runaway from the subscriber a Negro MAN named Peter Long, about six feet high, toks good English - Had on when he went away, a light colour'd homespun Coat, knit jacket and dark brown Breeches, is about 25 Years of Age. - Whoever will take up said Negro, and confine him in any of his Majesty's Gaols, so that he may be had, or return him to his Master, shall have Ten Dollows Reward and necessary Charges paid by Marifield Berry. Rye, October 16, 1775.[28]

"Paul, (a black man)" is reported to have enlisted in the war as early as July 1776 with Capt. Samuel Nay's Company in Col Joshua Wingate's Regiment. He was stationed at Fort Ticonderoga, in Col. David Gilman's Regiment and fought at Trenton and Princeton. Finally, with 121 North Hampton men led by Col. Alexander Scammell, in April 1777 he fought at Saratoga, in Capt. Richard Weare's Company.[29]

Paul was discharged in 1781 and he returned to North Hampton. Three years later, he married Phebe Swain and in 1789, Paul, Betty, and Alice Long, children of Paul and Phebe, were baptized in the church.[30] It is possible (but not certain) that Paul and Phebe had as many as five children: Paul, date of birth unknown (perhaps 1785); Nancy, born in 1792; Elizabeth (also Betsy or Betty), date of birth unknown (perhaps 1789); Alice, born 1787; and Deborah, born 1800. Alice and Nancy's deaths are also recorded in church records in North Hampton. They died a few months apart in 1804 from consumption, Alice, age seventeen and Nancy, just twelve years old. In 1805, Betsy (Long) Cummings died of consumption. She was the wife of James, and third child of Paul and Phebe. Then, Paul's wife, Phebe's death is recorded at age fifty in 1818. Paul died suddenly in 1826 at age seventy-four, having lost his wife and two daughters. His pension document states that he had become totally blind by 1820 and had been surviving through support of the Town of North Hampton.[31] Only Deborah Long survived until age seventy. She died in 1871 with this notation, "a Christian - sick for many years." Consumption seems to have claimed most of Paul Long's family as well as Alice Long's family.

In 1823, Rev. French, pastor of the North Hampton Congregational Church, wrote "An Account of Citizens of North Hampton - Where they Live." In this piece, he names three blacks still living near mills, which belonged to the Jenness, Seavey, and Wallis families. The blacks are William Scott, Alice Long's husband, Caesar Jenness and Paul Long.[32]

Cesar Small

"Cesar Small, A Mulatto, between 50 & 60 yrs of age, [died April 21, 1777] of Camp Distemper."[33]

Cesar is not listed in the church record as belonging to anyone, so he may have lived in Hampton as a free man. Cato Small, "of black complexion," is also known to have served in the Continental Army in Colonel Davis's regiment, but was engaged by the town of Sutton, New Hampshire, in 1781 for three years in order to fulfill their enlistment quota. He was seventeen years old at the time and may have been related to Cesar and Dinah Small, but Cato is not listed in Hampton records.[34]

A record of black soldiers in the Revolutionary War indicates that Cesar Small served, enlisting in the company of Capt. Samuel Nay. It was into Col. Joshua Wingate's regiment that he went first to Fort Ticonderoga in 1776 to help other black soldiers fortify the fort.[35] Only a year later, Hampton's historian, Joseph Dow, claims that Cesar "died from exposure in the army."[36]

Cesar enlisted, perhaps, because he and Dinah were warned out of Hampton in 1774.[37] Being "warned out" of a town meant that you were in significant financial need and the town looked upon you as a drain on their small resources for sheltering, feeding, and clothing residents. If this were true in Cesar Small's case, enlisting was one way for a black man to receive an income that could sustain himself and others. If Cesar died in combat, however, he would have left his relatives both impoverished and without his means of support. Cesar's wife or sister, Dinah Small, may formerly have been the slave of William Godfrey of North Hampton. After Cesar's death, however, in 1777, Dinah married Philip Burdoo who is said to have been a slave of Jonathan Moulton's. Dinah (Small) Burdoo and Philip shared quite a life together, but Dinah Burdoo came back to Hampton to live near the end of her life until her death in 1825. (Read more of Dinah's story below.)

Philip Burdoo

Philip Burdoo is said to have been a slave of Jonathan Moulton's.[38]

The Burdoo family that Dinah Small married into is believed to have been a family of free blacks in Massachusetts. The Burdoo family history begins with the marriage of Philip's grandfather, Philip Burdoo Sr., "who lived on the Bedford Road nearly opposite the Simonds Tavern" to Ann Solomon in 1704.[39] They settled in Lexington where Philip Sr. appears in the 1729 tax valuation. Early in their marriage, Philip and Ann may have lived at just below the average income of a Lexington, Massachusetts landowner. We know this by the number of horses, cows, oxen, and pigs that were declared in that 1729 document. One huge advantage for Philip as a free black is that he could own his own home. It was in this home that Philip and Ann raised six children. They were: Philip Jr. (b.1709); Eunice, (a twin, died 1720); Moses (b.1710), who served in the French and Indian War; Aaron (b.1712); Phineas (b.1715), who died unmarried in 1766, and Lois (b.1720). Lois was baptized and admitted to full Communion in 1742 in Bedford, Massachusetts. Philip Sr. died in 1750.

Philip Jr. (b.1709), first-born and twin, lived on or near his father's farm. There is one "rambling tale" that recounts a 1760 fur-trading trip that Philip made to upstate New York with a man named Edmund Monroe. Perhaps it was then that Philip Jr. began to imagine a place where his children might settle someday as free men and women. Philip was thought of as a yeoman and may have hired himself out as a laborer to area residents. He married Mary and with her had children: Philip (b. 1738), who married Dinah Small and lived in Hampton; Mary (b. 1740); and Silas (b. 1748), a well-known Revolutionary soldier who, after the war, settled in Reading, Vermont. Silas's post war life in Reading included two marriages but no children. Philip and Mary had a fourth child, unnamed, who died in 1755. In the 1771 tax valuation Philip Jr. is listed as not owning but sharing property with James Wisman. His son, Silas, is also listed not as owning land but living as neighbor to Prince Stone, who was a freed slave of Samuel Stone.

Dinah Small Burdoo

Dinah Small Burdoo, wife of Philip Burdoo, (son of Philip Jr.) was considered by Hampton historian Joseph Dow, "among the last of the old-time Negros in this town." Dinah Small was perhaps a widow or sister of Cesar Small, who died from exposure in the army in 1777. She married Philip Burdoo (b. 1738), who hailed from Moultonborough on January 9, 1783.[40] Rev. Ebenezer Thayer officiated at the ceremony and in his long list of weddings over the course of his ministry, the recording of Philip and Dinah's wedding stands out. Nearly every other wedding that is recorded uses the titles "Mr." for the groom and "Miss" or "Mrs." for the bride. When Rev. Thayer recorded this wedding it reads: "Philip Burdoo and Dinah Small," with neither name being preceded by a title of any kind.

It has been asserted that they were both slaves of General Jonathan Moulton, which may have been true of Philip, who came from one of the townships granted to the general. Dinah, however, certainly was the slave of William Godfrey, of North Hampton. Godfrey's granddaughter, Mrs. Fanny Lane, wrote of Dinah's service for the Godfrey family.[41] Beginning in 1792, Philip was employed for a time at the Leavitt Tavern in Hampton near his home. The tavern was later purchased and renamed Dearborn Inn.

In the 1790 census, Philip and Dinah are listed as living in Hampton as freed slaves. Philip died January 6, 1806. In the Hampton Town Records dated March 11, 1806, there are three entries that offer the details of Philip's care at the end of his life:

The town paid $1.00 for "digging Philip Burdoo's grave," $1.07 for "sundries for Mrs. Burdoo," and $3.81 for "sundries for Philip Burdoo." The town also paid $2.00 to "Mrs. Rendell taking care of Philip Burdoo" and $1.33 to Jeremiah Hobbs for "making coffin for Philip Burdoo." Finally, the Town paid Doctor Lawrence $18.00 for "doctoring Philip Burdoo," $2.00 was paid to Samuel Sanborn for "work, etc for Philip Burdoo," and $1.00 to John Green for "wood for Mrs. Burdoo." [42]

Philip's death left Dinah living in a house a few rods east of the Centre School where she spun, knitted, and lived contentedly. When she became enfeebled by age, she was cared for by the town and died at Deacon John Lamprey's on January 11, 1825, at ninety-two years of age. In 1809, John Dow, James Leavitt and Jonathan Marston Jr. were chosen for a committee to take the whole matter of Dinah's condition and support into consideration. They reported at some length on individual cases, and this pertains to Dinah's situation:

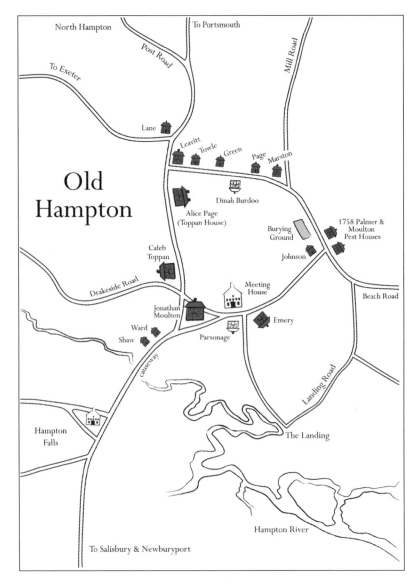

Map of Old Hampton showing the approximate location of Dinah Burdoo's house. Map courtesy of Cheryl Lassiter, graphic artist and local author.

As it respects Mrs. Burdoo, considering her advanced aged and her exposedness to take cold if she continue in her house, and the expense of hauling her wood, we think it best to put her in a family, where she can be taken proper care of till spring. Mr. Josiah Dearborn has offered to take her at four shillings per week. She has been at Mr. Dearborn's house about a fortnight.[43]

Her death was marked in the church record thus:

Mrs. Dinah Bourdoo, colored woman, (died) aged, as is supposed, 92, Lung difficulty. Sudden. Till this time she retained her powers of body and mind almost perfectly. Not a professor, but serious, undoubtedly more worthy than many professors.[44]

Dinah shared the admiration of Rev. Josiah Webster at her death with Alice Page, both of whom were lauded for their worth, which lay beyond that of many professors.

One might wonder why Dinah was left to fend for herself near the end of her life, rather than to be taken in by one of her Burdoo family members. Unfortunately, the Burdoo family story suggests the struggle that free blacks faced, as the century progressed, to hold on to their place in society. Philip Sr. had prospered and eventually reached what we might call "the middle class" of Lexington farmers. They joined the church and had enjoyed the same civic rights and obligations as their white neighbors. Moses Burdoo had been able to bring suit—and win—before the county justice of the peace. Despite the Massachusetts ban on Negroes—slave or free—bearing arms, the Burdoos joined the provincial militia and fought in the French and Indian War.[45] Yet, even with this early societal acceptance the family experienced hard times after the Revolutionary War.

They lost their property and by the time Dinah needed their help, they were as impoverished as she.

Although not included in any documents from Hampton, below is a brief sketch of Philip Burdoo's other free, black relatives. Their tales offer an unusual glimpse into a family where slavery was neither the dominating cultural force that drove their choices nor the determiner of the consequences of their actions.

Moses Burdoo

Moses (b. 1710), uncle of Philip Burdoo, lived in the Lexington, Massachusetts area. There are records of "wages owed" to him and he sued a Mr. Jonas Whittaker of Concord, Massachusetts, for an unpaid debt plus the cost of the legal proceedings. He won the suit.[46] Another record from 1742 concerns a fornication case that was brought against Hannah Hammond, a free black woman from Middlesex County, Massachusetts. Hannah was one of the last women of color who was taken to court for a charge of fornication. She was indicted by the grand jury and asked to speak to her crime. It was the usual case to inquire as to the name of the father and in this case, Hannah named Moses Burdoo of Lexington County, Massachusetts. Moses' race was not listed nor was his occupation. (Not even his birth certificate lists his race.) Hannah was fined a pound for her crime even though her child died. Moses was not fined by the court, which was typical in such cases of that time.[47]

In 1754, Moses married Phebe Bannister of Concord, Massachusetts. They had Eli and Moses Jr., who were baptized in 1755, before Phebe died in 1756. Moses, so early widowed, enlisted and served in the French and Indian War, fighting in Canada. Moses' will of 1759 survives and indicates that it was written during his enlistment. He left his body in "the hands of Lt. Abijah Smith to be decently Buried if it shall please Almighty God to take me out of the World while I Remain

under his Command."[48] Moses actually died in 1784. Moses'
son, Eli, later appears on the poor list of the town of Lexington,
Massachusetts. However, Eli, along with his cousin, Silas (son
of Philip Jr.) participated in the Revolutionary War as soldiers
who enlisted from Lexington, Massachusetts. In 1775, Silas
was twenty-seven years old, a free black man who lived in
Lexington and Cambridge alternately, but owned no Lexington
property. Eli was twenty years old, also a free black man from
Lexington, Massachusetts. It appears that Dinah and Philip
were not involved in caring for Eli or Moses Jr. between 1756,
when Phebe died, and 1784, when Moses died, despite Moses'
enlistment.

Aaron Burdoo

Aaron, uncle of Philip Burdoo, was born in 1712 and appears
on the 1774 tax list for Lexington. He must have been truly
poor for he possessed almost no land. Aaron had a child, Aaron
(b. 1745). In the records of the Lexington Church, an Aaron
Burdoo is listed as having been baptized and received into the
church in 1780. It is unclear whether this was father or son, but
I assume it was the son because he appears in Reading, Vermont,
in 1794. Aaron married first, Phebe Lew, freeborn, (b. 1745) of
Groton, Massachusetts, in 1788. Phebe Lew was the daughter
of Primus Slave (b. 1715) and Margaret Lew (b. 1720). Phebe's
brother, Barzillai, also freeborn, served in the French and Indian
War as well as the Revolutionary War. Records indicate that
several children were born to Phebe and Aaron and that the
family was quite respected.

Rebecca Dexter was Aaron's second wife, whom he married
in Reading, Vermont, in 1821. First Congregational Church
records from Windsor, Vermont, show a Rebecca Burdoo joining
in 1843 by letter from Reading. Children of Rebecca and Aaron
are: Aaron (b. 1822), Silas (b. 1826), and Philip (b. 1828). Silas

lived in Woodstock, Vermont, and was said to have had the largest library in the area. He served in the Civil War. May Grace Canfield, Vermont author and historian, wrote, "In the Ralph yard are buried...Silas Burdoo, a colored man, who served in the war between the States and lived in the Ralph-Walker family, rests here."[49] Within the last five years, the current owners of the Walker home were digging near the house in the midst of a remodeling. They discovered a slave collar but there are no indications as to whom it belonged. Silas died having worked as a farm hand for the Walker family for forty-three years and was described as "faithful, intelligent and industrious."[50]

There is an intestate record for Aaron dated 1831 in the files of the Windsor, Vermont District Probate Court. It lists Aaron's inventory as including a small and large Bible and a *History of New England*, as well as *Carver's Travels*, all totaling almost two hundred dollars. His widow, Rebecca, was given most of this property to sell. Her death is recorded as 1846.

Moses Burdoo (son of Philip's brother, Moses)

In 1778 Moses Burdoo (born 1753), married Lois Ralf of Boston, Massachusetts. In the 1790 U.S. Census, a Lois Burdoo is listed as head of household, living in Jaffrey, New Hampshire, with six other free persons. Town records for Jaffrey indicate a Moses Burdoo, blacksmith, consenting to a petition pleading against setting off a portion of the town of Jaffrey, as of May 1787, but no record beyond this date.[51] Moses and Lois had children: Polly (1778–1794), who died at the home of Amos Fortune; Moses (b. 1780); Philip (b. 1783); and Sally (b. 1785). Lois and her children were supported by the town after Moses' death sometime between 1787 and 1790 as Dinah had been supported in Hampton. However, two of Lois's children met sad fates, made less sad by Amos Fortune.

Amos Fortune was a prince of the At-mun-shi tribe and

was born in Africa in 1710. In 1725, he was captured by slave traders and it is said that he bore the sign of the whip that was used on his back, received when he tried to save his sister from the same fate. Amos's first owner was a Quaker from Massachusetts, Caleb Copeland. Because Caleb did not believe in slavery, he planned to free Amos as soon as he could read and write and make a living.

Amos learned weaving and when Mr. Copeland first offered him his freedom, he refused, saying he was not ready. He had seen the extreme poverty of other freed slaves and Amos did not want to choose that as his fate. Before he could be freed, however, his owner died and Amos was sold along with Caleb's other belongings to cover the family debt. Ichabod Richardson bought Amos and held him as slave for the next twenty years. When Ichabod died, his wife wrote, "In consideration of the many faithful services Amos Fortune did perform...I do grant Amos Fortune full and free liberty of his person." This piece of paper never left Amos's person thereafter.[52]

In the following years, Amos settled in Jaffrey, New Hampshire, where he helped two African women, Violet and Celyndia, gain their freedom. He took up the trade of tanner and at age eighty, bought his own land upon which he built a house and barn. Shortly afterward, the town of Jaffrey passed a resolution "not to raise money for the eight children and widows, white and black, from families too poor to feed themselves."[53] Rather, these women and children were to be auctioned off to work in exchange for food and shelter. Amos could not stand the thought of selling children after all he had done trying to save his own sister. So, he used his savings to purchase one of the children about to be auctioned, Polly Burdoo.

Polly Burdoo, age fourteen, and Moses Burdoo, age twelve, were to be auctioned off as slaves. Since Polly was often sick as a child, Amos Fortune bid on her for one pound sixteen. Amos took Polly home and although she died within the year, the town paid Amos for her care. Amos married the widow Lois Burdoo in 1793 when he took Polly into his home. Moses, Polly's brother, was sold to Joseph Stewart to be held until he turned twenty-one years of age. Lois died in 1847, but not before she and Amos had taken many needy children into their home. Before he died, in 1801, Amos used his last savings, which amounted to $243, to set up a fund to be used to educate all children, black or white, to know what freedom and dignity meant for all people.[54] It is ironic to think that the fate of a member of the once prosperous Burdoo family should be made more merciful by another freed African American man nearly one hundred years after Philip Burdoo Sr. first settled on his family farm.

Cato (Moulton), "Elijah Barlet"

Cato had been bought and sold several times before being owned by Jonathan Moulton. Cato preferred the name of Elijah Bartlet, stating that this was "his right name."[55] The following advertisement makes a reference to Cato being born in New York State. Since New York's first slave owners dated to 1646, it could well have been that a family of Bartletts were Cato's first owners, but obviously not his last:

> The New England Chronicle (Boston) January 18 to January 25, 1776 offers a $15 reward for a run away from Col. Jonathan Moulton (October last - 1775) a Negro boy named Cato, about 18 years of age, 5 ft and ½ inch – a strait limb'd, well-built and active boy, and plays well on a fife. He is very apt to scowl or knit his brows and has had the small-pox by inoculation, which he shows but little in his face. But the place on his arm where he was inoculated is plain to be discovered. Since he ran away he was taken up

at Durham, and in conveying him to his master he made his escape. Since that he was at headquarters, and offered to inlist, but not meeting with success, he went from thence to Lexington, where he offered his service to Mr. John Buckman, innholder in that town and called himself Elijah Bartlet. He said that he was free born. Mr. Buckman suspecting him to be a runaway, which the boy perceiving, he stopped but a few days and went off privately, which was some time in November last. His master has had no intelligence of him since. He had on when he went away, a blue duffel round jacket, with cuff, and without lining, a blue large jacket, both almost new and a pair of leather breeches, and carried with him 3 check shirts, 2 of which were cotton and woolen and the other linen, with large checks &c, but it appears he has exchanged some of his outside cloaths for other of another colour. Whoever will take him said runaway and convey him to his master, or secure him in any way of the colony goals, so that his master can have him again, shall have $15 and all necessary charges paid by JONA MOULTON Hampton, January 1, 1776.

N.B. As the boy was born at New York and from some other reasons it's likely he is thence making his way; but it's more likely he will offer himself to work by the month or year, in some part of the colony of Massachusetts Bay or Connecticut and whoever may have the opportunity of taking up said runaway is cautioned to take particular care lest he makes his escape again as he is so artful and cunning a boy."[56]

Runaway slaves were almost a fact of life for most slave owners. Most ran away for short terms to avoid the dreadful monotony of continual work or to avoid punishment. Fugitives were a different matter. They meant to escape their bondage altogether. It was easier to be a fugitive if you had lived in New England for a time, spoke English and at least had some sense of direction. But oftentimes a slave would have little knowledge of the geography, the severe range of climate, or in which direction to travel to reach a "free territory." But run they did, again and again aiming for that "state of freedom" and while they were on the run, ads would also run in the local newspapers. It is surprising what the tone of an ad would reveal. Not only is there a complete lack of understanding or empathy toward the condition of servitude, but most masters focused on the inconvenience to themselves.

Cato, while still a runaway, could not enlist in the service. This meant that he would likely need to survive by loaning out his services as a husbander or laborer. Captain Moulton would have every wish to have him home, however. His first wife, Abigail, had died of small pox and Jonathan Moulton wished to marry again. His plan was to bring his new wife into his household, and Cato's presence would have certainly made her transition easier. It could have been Captain Moulton who said as George Washington did, "The running off of my cook has been a most inconvenient thing to this family." From Cato's perspective, however, even the alternative of military service must have looked much more attractive than being "broken in again" to a new mistress's whims and schedules. So, Cato kept running until he bumped into Mr. John Buckman.

Mr. Buckman was correct to be cautious about "Elijah Bartlet" when he offered his services at his tavern. To accept a stranger into your family was to make a statement, in the eyes of the town selectmen, that you would become financially responsible for this stranger. If a family did not keep this pledge, the guest would have been asked by the town to leave—a practice called "warning out." A tavern owner would have wanted to avoid the impression that he could not keep his house in order and may have also wanted to avoid any legal entanglements that ensued when the master discovered his runaway.

Cato must have eventually been returned or returned on his own since in September 1776 he enlisted as a fifer in Captain William Prescott's company in Colonel Thomas Tash's regiment of militia. He served at or near Fort Ticonderoga and may have been part of action near Trenton and Princeton, both in New Jersey. If, indeed, he was at these sites, he saw very heavy fighting.

Of all the deterrents against running away, the most controversial were the fugitive slave laws. In 1643, the New England Confederation had made a pact between the colonies and got agreement for the return of fugitive slaves. During the Revolution, this pact was re-evaluated and in 1787, a new ordinance provided that "any person escaping into the Northwest Territory from whom labor or service is lawfully claimed in any one of the original states, such fugitive may be lawfully reclaimed and conveyed to the person claiming his or her labor or service aforesaid."[57] Making this law was probably easier that enforcing it. The closer the colonies came to the dawn of the nineteenth century, the more free states were created and the more contradictions arose between the states about how to arrest, detain, and prosecute those who were caught.

Caesar (Moulton)

Caesar Moulton was also a slave of General Jonathan Moulton. His time of enslavement overlapped with that of Cato's. Not as much information is available about Caesar and he does not appear in the church record. But we do have an idea of some of the work that Cato and Caesar were asked to do for this master who was an industrious, prominent citizen and somewhat of a schemer and adventurer.

The following story reveals Moulton's skill at bartering and obviously comes from a time in his life where his energies were still focused on acquiring and not losing things that were precious to him.

After obtaining a grant for the lands that became Moulton-borough and Center Harbor, the colonel was not yet sufficiently satisfied in his passion for land ownership. He decided on a plan to acquire a bit more land by using a little flattery in naming his son Benning, for Governor Benning Wentworth of New Hampshire. Then, he sent his two slaves, Cato and Caesar, to Governor Wentworth. They had been directed to hang a garland of flowers around the neck of a 1400-pound ox, put roses over his back, and hang a flag on his horns, which they did. They then led the ox to Portsmouth and presented him to his Excellency Governor Benning Wentworth with the compliments of Colonel Moulton. "On receiving this gift the governor asked what the Colonel would like for compensation, but was told nothing unless the governor would be willing to give him 'a gore of land' which contained 19,422 acres of land, a part of which constituted what is now New Hampton."[58] So General Moulton acquired a third town by wit and imagination but not without the labor of his slaves, and the very real risk to their lives of marching that 1400 pound ox from Hampton to Portsmouth.

Dinah Whipple (Chase/Wingate)

"Dinah, Servant to Widow Chase" [owned the covenant and was admitted to full communion on February, 28, 1779][59]

Joshua Wingate built a beautiful home that in later years became known as "the old Toppan House" after it was handed down from Joshua to his grandson, Colonel Christopher Toppan. Christopher's father, Dr. Edmund Toppan, had married Sarah Wingate. Colonel Christopher's son, Edmund, also married a Wingate relative, Mary Chase, who was the granddaughter of Rev. Stephen and Jane (Wingate) Chase. Paine Wingate became the storyteller of the Wingates. Paine tells of seeing in his grandfather's house "the lingering existence of slavery in New England."[60] He is most probably referring to Dinah Chase and perhaps Peter Chase, who both were slaves in the Wingate household. The Congregational Church records for North Hampton Church as kept by Nathaniel Gookin Jr. mention on October 15, 1752, the baptism of "Dinah, Negro of Colonel Wingate's" and on October 3, 1779, the baptism of "Peter, Servant of John Wingate."[61]

Paine Wingate's aunt, Jane (Wingate) Chase, who was the wife of Rev. Stephen Chase of New Castle, might have brought Dinah Chase into her family by way of marriage to Stephen. If this is so, then we can imagine that "Dinah, negro of Col. Wingate's" is the Dinah (Chase) Whipple who is named in the following paragraph as belonging to Rev. Stephen Chase of New Castle, and subsequently moving to Hampton with him in 1779.

Rev. Chase moved to Hampton during the Revolutionary War and took Dinah (probably Dinah "Wingate") with him. She was admitted to the church under the tutelage of Rev. Dr. Ebenezer Thayer at about seventeen years of age.[62] There is little known about her life or her relationship to the church over the next four years. We pick up Dinah's story again when she turns twenty-one, is freed, and moves to Portsmouth to marry Prince Whipple, February 22, 1781, in North Church. It is said that on Dinah and Prince's wedding day that William Whipple prepared a certain document that allowed Prince the rights of a free man. The same was true for Dinah, in that Rev. Chase freed her on her wedding day. What this freedom meant for Prince is unclear because the date of his formal manumission is not until February 26, 1784. It may have been that the clergyman who married them requested such documentation to satisfy his mind that this marriage ritual solemnized a union between two free individuals in the eyes of God.

In any case, Dinah and Prince began married life by moving in with Cuffee Whipple and Rebecca Deverson. Cuffee was perhaps brother or cousin to Prince and their ancestor was likely a king from the Gold Coast of Africa. Prince had been the property of General William Whipple and Katherine Moffatt. After General Whipple's death, Mrs. Whipple gave Cuffee and Prince a lot behind her house, which was where they lived, in a small, two-story house where living quarters were tight for two couples. Prince and Cuffee were music makers and Dinah taught school in the home. Her school was likely the Ladies Charitable African School and it existed until 1850. The house grew fuller as Dinah and Prince's daughters, Esther and Elizabeth, were born and joined the several children Dinah taught. Not unlike the present-day circumstances for some families living paycheck to paycheck, Dinah and her wider family needed the occasional help of the Portsmouth church, especially after she was widowed. Found in the Portsmouth Athenaeum, recorded in a small, softcover book, is a list of charitable distributions, mostly to women, who belonged to the Portsmouth North Church, including a record of the help that the church offered to Dinah, Rebecca, Prince, Cuffee, and others. This list is contained all on the same page, with the quotation marks coming from the original:

> "Cuff Whipple" (1803, May 4)
> "Widow P Whipple" (1805 Sep 12, 1806 Apr 18);
> "Phillis" (1810 Nov, Dec)
> "Prince Whipple's Family" (1811 Apr)
> "Paid for Phillis' funeral" and "Paid to Dinah"
>   (1811 Jun 18)

"Cuffee's Widow"- (1818 Dec) [This would be Rebecca
    Daverson]
"Dinah Whipple" (1818 Dec)
"Mrs. Francis" (Coloured) (1818 Dec)
"Dinah Whipple" (1819 Dec)
"Cuffee's Widow" (1819 Dec)
"1820 Aug 7: Dinah Whipple pd $2.00; Mrs. Barnard
    pd. $3.00"
[c.1820-21 Feb 1, Feb 26: Dinah Whipple signed
    document:] "Deacon Tappan is please to let me have
    one dollar for to get some wood" (sic) She got wood
    twice, $1 each time, plus .25.
1820 Aug 2: "Dinah Whipple, Mrs. Barnard both paid by
    the church"[63]

During all of the years between Dinah's tutelage by Rev. Thayer
and her owning the covenant in 1779, until 1821, twenty-five
years after Prince's death, Dinah remained in the record book at
Hampton as a member. In 1821, in July, during the pastorate
of Rev. Josiah Webster, there is this note recorded "Voted, that
Dinah Chase, a member of this Chh [shorthand for "church"]
now resident at Portsmouth, be permitted to unite with the first
Chh in Portsmouth and that such union with that Chh be her
dismission from the first Chh of Christ in this town."[64]

Of Prince and Dinah's children, we know little, except that
their daughter, Esther Whipple married a Mr. Mullinaux and
lived not far from Dinah. Dinah was widowed in 1796 and in
1816, Rebecca, Dinah's sister-in-law, was also widowed. Dinah
lived at a home on High Street in Portsmouth until 1832 and
then moved to Pleasant Street for fourteen years. She died in
1846 at eighty-six years of age. North Church of Portsmouth
paid $8.62 for her funeral and Eben Lord made her coffin.
Esther's house, upon her death in 1868, went to Leonard

Cotton, a sixty-eight-year-old merchant from Washington Street. Prince Whipple and his daughter, Esther Mullinaux, are buried in North Burying Ground on Maplewood Ave. in Portsmouth.[65] It is believed that Esther saw to having Dinah buried near Prince.

Neb Miller (Toppan)

"Neb Miller, a Negro slave of Colonel Christopher Toppan."[66]

Neb Miller's name does not appear in the record books of the church. He may or may not have been related to Jonathan and Robert Miller, both men of color who resided in Hampton Falls, sons of Robert Miller Sr. He may have been purchased during the days that Christopher Toppan was trading with the West Indies. Since Mr. Toppan sailed his first ship at eighteen, he could have purchased a slave like Neb as early as 1753. Colonel Christopher Toppan was the fourth child of Dr. Edmund Toppan. He married Sarah Parker of Portsmouth. Christopher died in 1818 at age eighty-three. Sarah lived nearly another twenty years until she died in 1837. Their daughter, Sarah, married Rev. Nathaniel Thayer, son of Ebenezer Thayer, one of the pastors at First Congregational Church, Hampton. Christopher was a fisherman and shipbuilder and had grown up in the care of his mother's brother-in-law, Rev. Nathaniel Gookin. No evidence was found which might reveal whether or not Neb shared in the fishing or ship building. It would not be outside the realm of possibility since such tasks involved hours of mending nets, varnishing, sanding, polishing, and other time-consuming but not difficult tasks.

Two stories remain about Neb Miller, Christopher Toppan's slave. They are told by Lucy Ellen Dow, daughter of Joseph Dow, historian and compiler of much of the genealogy of early Hampton residents. Here, she has captured a couple of light-hearted moments that reveal humorous pranks which may or may not have come with the risk of punishment after the fact:

> The Colonel was especially fond of pigeon shooting. A pigeon stand consisted of a pole resting horizontally on two crotched stakes, two or three tame pigeons for hoverers and fliers, and a net-house—a little hut of evergreen boughs within which the gunner sat concealed. The hoverers were blinded and placed on frames, to be seesawed from behind the screen; a long line was tied around the leg of the flier; the man crept into the net-house, cocked his gun and waited. When a flock was seen approaching, the flier was deftly tossed into the air to the length of its line, where it swayed and fluttered, then gently settled back, and the strange birds came and alighted on the pole to make acquaintance. Now was the supreme moment for the sportsman, who deemed himself unlucky if less than half-a-dozen fell victims to his shot. Col. Toppan's negro servant, Neb Miller, dearly loved a practical joke; and, one morning, being sent ahead with the decoys, the temptation was too strong to be resisted, to take out the charge from the gun, replace a single shot, ram back the wad, and set the gun in its accustomed place. A little later, the unsuspecting Colonel, seeing an especially fine opportunity to display his skill, fired; but when only one pigeon fell, his chagrin was almost too great to bear.

The second story is a bit more gastronomical:

> This [same] Neb Miller had once too long-continued a diet of porridge to suit his taste; and so, to end it, he contrived to open a hole down from the

chamber above, over the kitchen fireplace, and to have a line with a slip-noose ready for action; then, watching his chance, he slipped the noose around the short leg of the kettle, tipped it over and drew up the line. When Neb was called down to breakfast, the cook was in great consternation about a kettle of porridge, spread over the floor; and for that morning at least, there was no porridge for breakfast.[67]

If Neb Miller was related to Jonathan and Robert Miller of Hampton Falls, which at this time remains unconfirmed, you can learn more about that particular Miller family later in this work.

Ben Thompson (Marston)

"Ben Thompson, slave of Captain Jonathan Marston."[68]

Ben Thompson does not appear in the church record and such records rarely indicate how a slave such as Ben Thompson came to be owned by someone. It is said that Captain Marston's father, Elisha, who established the Marston homestead, gave each of his children a slave. If this is true, then Elisha would have owned at least six slaves. However, the probate record that Elisha left, although it takes great pain to divide his not insignificant land holdings among his family members, does not mention that any slaves were passed on to Elisha's children and does not refer to Ben Thompson by name. Since Elisha died in 1762, Jonathan (third-oldest son) was still only ten years old and not old enough—twenty-one—to own land or property. When Captain Jonathan Marston (b. 1752) did come of age, he married Lydia Robinson of Exeter in 1780 and settled on property across the street from his father's homestead. They had nine children, but among the writings about this family nothing is yet known to give us any broader picture of who Ben Thompson may have been or what work he may have been required to accomplish.

There are two other African American men named Thompson who were known to have served in the Revolutionary War: Caesar, who hailed from Concord, New Hampshire, and Prince, whose enlistment lists that he came from Canterbury, New Hampshire. Not much beyond their military records is known about either Prince or Caesar. There is even a Benjamin Thompson listed (ethnicity uncertain) as having served in the Revolutionary War from the state of Massachusetts, who was sick and mustered out after a year of being unable to do his duty. Consequently, Ben, Caesar and Prince—all named Thompson— could have had no blood ties at all, or the three could have been brothers. Historical records, such as this one in Joseph Dow's history of Hampton, are so slim as to be both tantalizing and frustrating all at once and a clear reminder that no one's life can be summed up in one phrase.

Phillis White

"Phyllis White, black woman" [died August 14, 1830].[69]

"Phillis White, colored, widow of Archelaus, died August 14, 1830. The graves of Phillis White and three other Negros, probably her family, are in a field belonging to Mr. Aiken S. Coffin."[70]

Archelaus White was born in New Ipswich, New Hampshire, in 1757 and was the slave of James White of Plaistow. In his application for military service, he listed himself as "farmer." Archelaus was one of several black soldiers who settled in Exeter, New Hampshire, in the "New Guinea" area after serving as a private in the Revolutionary War. He had fought at Bunker Hill with Capt. Jeremiah Gilman and been present at the capture of General Burgoyne before being discharged in Bethlehem, New Jersey. Archelaus was one of a small handful of black soldiers who were originally rejected when they made application to local New Hampshire officials and had to turn to Massachusetts for their first service in the war.[71]

After the war was over, Rev. John Murray of Newburyport, Massachusetts, officiated at the marriage of Archelaus and Phillis Shepherd on May 29, 1783. In the 1790 census of non-white families, Archelaus White is listed as head of household in Exeter, and he has another non-white living with him whom one may presume is his wife, Phillis.[72] Archelaus and Phillis rented for a time from lawyer Oliver Peabody in Exeter after the war ended.[73] Because Dow's history of the White family suggests that there may be other family members buried near Phillis White's grave, besides Archelaus, it is easy to speculate as to whether some of the other Whites listed in various other records might be children of Phillis and Archelaus. There is a Levi White listed in the 1790 census as a free non-white person living in Londonderry with five persons in his family. Levi may have been a brother of Archelaus. Later, in the early to mid-1800s, we find this statement:

> On March 5, 1849, Rockingham County billed the town of Derry for Jane White and Catherine White [listed as Negro] for board and clothing for a year at $57.75 and $55.01 respectively.

On February 6, 1850, "a colored man," Joseph L. White, boarding at Exeter was "given supplies in wood ($17.25), house rent ($11.38) and provisions ($8.00).[74]

There is no verification that Joseph, Levi, Jane or Catherine are related to Phillis and Archelaus. They are, however, the only non-white "Whites" who were listed in any census or pauper list in the wider Exeter area. Archelaus was eligible to apply for a pension by virtue of his service in the Revolutionary War. There is a record of his pension application and in it Archelaus is described by his former master, James White, as "now very infirm and extremely poor."[75]

One might assume from his pension record statement that James White freed Archelaus after his service in the Revolutionary War. Joseph Dow's history of Hampton as it relates to Phillis, names her as "colored widow" so she may well have been a free or freed African woman as well when she married Archelaus.

Archelaus's death is listed as 1826 in Exeter. This likely means that neither he nor Phillis received more than a pittance from his pension. From the record it appears that Phillis White died four years after Archelaus, in 1830, in Hampton. She may have worshiped at the church, but never joined, since there is no record of her becoming a member. After her death, Mr. Aiken Coffin offers his field as a resting place for the White family. Phillis may have sought refuge with Mr. Coffin because of her extreme poverty for it seems that in the four years after Archelaus's death she received only $38.45 in pension payments prior to her own death. Alternately, Mr. Coffin may have been a member of a small group of deacons or elders who were tasked to care for Phillis as Deacon Lamprey and others had cared for Dinah Burdoo until her death in 1826. Mr. Aiken Coffin's farm and mill were situated not far from the present-day Hurd farm. Mr. Aiken's mill took advantage of the stream that flows under the bridge connecting Hampton and Hampton Falls and there, also, the White family received Mr. Aiken's generosity in providing their final resting place.

By caring for Phillis, Mr. Coffin also saved the town of Hampton certain expenses. Paupers, vagrants, and "idlers" were great risks to a Puritan community since the moral code of conduct required that the town in which such idlers were found was responsible for the care of them. From about 1659, Massachusetts had set the limit of occupancy in any given town at three months, after which a town was required to begin public relief. So a system known as "warning out" was adopted in both Massachusetts and throughout the colonies. A 1682 Massachusetts law defined the practice thus: "warning out means to banish any indigents, undesirables or idle persons suspected of becoming financial burdens upon the community." Often the selectmen would accompany the stranger or indigent person to the border of the next town in order to ascertain that the stranger had truly crossed over the town line. Warning out happened frequently to African American soldiers after the Revolution since the pension system for soldiers who had seen military action did not begin to pay out regularly until the early 1800s. Caesar Stevens (Caesar Black) of Kingston, for example, was not as lucky as the Whites. He was warned out of both Kingston and East Kingston as he made his way down the road seeking shelter and support.[76]

CHAPTER 7

Approaching the Revolution: The Service of African Americans

IN DELVING INTO THE records of slave-owning families that were part of First Congregational Church's journals, it was perhaps inevitable that other town families would also be revealed as slave-holding families in Hampton who neither baptized their slaves nor invited them to join First Congregational Church as members. They appeared in the history books simply as sellers, buyers, or inheritors of slaves; as neighbors of church members, business partners, or local men who were committed to different faith persuasions. Some of the names of these individuals are included below. Many of the families were also members of the First Congregational Church, many of them baptized and joined as members themselves. They simply did not include their slaves in these ecclesiastical practices. Although no church record survives of their slaves' names, these names appear in probated wills, pauper notices, or in the town lists of deaths, births, and marriages.

Kate (Dudley?/Marston?)

In the 1790 census, Jonathan Marston as head of household is noted as having one slave.[1] By 1790, most of the slaves who had been owned by Hampton families had gained their freedom. Kate is one of the last from Hampton who was not listed as "free, non-white" but still as "slave." There is nothing in the record to indicate that Kate belonged to either Jonathan Marston, head of the household, or his wife. However, Jonathan had married Lydia Robinson of Exeter, daughter of Josiah Robinson and Sarah Dudley. In October of 1753, Nicholas Dudley of Exeter (maternal grandfather of Lydia Marston) gave a receipt to his son-in-law Josiah Robinson (Lydia's father) and his daughter Sarah Dudley Robinson, (wife of said Josiah and mother of Lydia) for five pounds in full for a female "Negro Slave named Kate," then aged about eight years, which Josiah and Sarah bought from him. This receipt is written in a hand as smooth and clear as copperplate print. This autograph of Nicholas Dudley, which is perfectly plain, does indicate he could write.[2]

Nicholas Dudley died in 1766 and mentioned other slaves in his will and personal papers who were set free, but it may be that Kate is the "slave" who was given by Nicholas Dudley to Lydia's mother and father, who then gave Kate to their daughter at the time of her marriage in 1780. No paper trail verifies whether this was the case. It is reasonable to assume that Kate was still living with Jonathan and Lydia in 1790, for she would have been about forty-five years old. Since Jonathan and Lydia had nine children and he was a captain in the Revolutionary War, he would have been gone for a number of years, leaving Lydia and Kate to run the household and raise the children. The receipt gives no other information other than this woman is named Kate and that she was not free as late as 1790. As noted earlier, Ben Thompson appears in the Hampton history as a slave owned by Jonathan Marston. It is possible that Kate and Ben knew each other.

Unnamed "Negro man" (Hilliard or Hilyard)

"My wife to have my negro man untill my son Timothy Hilyard Comes to the age of twenty one years."

It is unfortunately the case that many times we know of an African person living within a community, but the record does not preserve a name. This is the case with Benjamin Hilliard's "Negro man." We know he existed, but we do not know his age, his physical, characteristics, nor his disposition. Because slave owners considered their slaves as possessions, the probate records often include the fact of a slave in the midst of a long, detailed list of possessions such as dishes, bowls, trunks, and great coats. That is the case in this 1723 record:

> I give and bequeath to my Loving wife Eleze-
> bath Hilyard the one third part of all my Land and
> marsh and my house and the half of my barn Roome
> and the one third of my movabls with in doars and
> the one third of my movabls with out doars and I
> give to my wife Elezibath Hilyard two hundred and
> Six pound Eight shillings and six pence in money or
> bills which was gave her by her father Joseph Chase
> and my wife to have my negro man untill my son
> Timothy Hilyard Comes to the age of twenty one
> years and then said negro to be my Son Timothy
> Hilyards and all my impliments of husbandry I give
> to my son Timothy Hilyard and at my wifes death or
> day of marriage my house and barn and Lands and
> marsh to Return to those my Children which I have
> gave them to in this my will and I doe make Consti-
> tute and Appoint my beLovid wife Elezebath Hilyard
> and my son Benjamin Hilyard to be my sole Execu-
> trix and Executor to this my Last will and Testiment
> Rattifieng and Confeirming this to be my Last will

and Testiment and no other in witnes here unto I the above named Benjamin Hilyard have here unto put my hand and seall."[3]

Benjamin Hilliard (1681–1723) was born and died in Hampton. He married first Mehitable Weare and married second Elizabeth Chase, but he was never a member of the church. Timothy Hilliard, the son mentioned in Benjamin's will, was born in 1713, also in Hampton, and died in 1745, in Chichester, New Hampshire. Timothy's probated will of 1745 does not reveal any slaves then owned by Timothy whom he bequeathed to any of his children. One can hope that the Negro man of Benjamin Hilliard was able to receive his freedom prior to Timothy's death.

Moses (Clough)

"Moses, a Lad presented by Jeremy Clough" [for baptism July 15, 1736].[4]

As part of the record left by Rev. Ward Cotton, there is listed this sentence about Moses, a lad presented by Jeremy Clough for baptism. The church record does not make reference to Moses as a Negro lad as it does in other places. Neither does the record state, "Moses, son of Jeremy" was brought for baptism. Therefore, it is assumed that Moses may have been a near relative of Jeremy's or an indentured servant. Deliverance Leavitt, Jeremy's wife, had been admitted to full Communion in April, just a few months prior to Moses' baptism, and she died October 31, aged 18 of throat ailment, just a few months afterward. There is no record that she and Jeremy bore a son, Moses.

Caesar Clough

A Caesar Clough, "black man," enlisted in the Revolutionary War in February 1778, serving in the company of Capt. Ezekiel

Worthen. He served in Rhode Island and when he enlisted a second time in March, he was near White Plains, New York. He claimed that he "hailed from Hampton, New Hampshire." In August, Caesar is reported as "sick" at Brunswick, New Jersey.[5] This is the extent of Caesar's military record, so there is a chance that he died of the sickness for which he reported. It is not known if Caesar Clough was related to Moses, or owned by Jeremy Clough or even freed by Jeremy Clough. A Caesar Clough did, however, marry a woman named Priscilla Glasgo in Exeter, December 9, 1777, both identified as "Negro."[6] This Caesar from Exeter, must be the same Caesar who enlisted and who married just before going into the army. Priscilla, who was known as "Cill" is believed to have married second, Primus Coffin, another black Revolutionary soldier in 1779.

Unknown "non-white"

Freed, non-white person living with Joseph Leach.[7]

Joseph Leach was a sergeant in the Revolutionary War and is listed in the 1790 Hampton census as head of household along with another free, non-white household member. Joseph was a ship carpenter and married Abigail Fifield (b. 1738). She was christened as an adult on 18 Aug 1754 in First Congregational Church, Hampton.[8] She married Joseph Leach about 1759, and her children include: Comfort, Molly, John, and Hannah, all baptized in the 1760s. The Leaches were a family of ship carpenters who worked at the Hampton shipyard.[9] So far, a name has not been found for the freed non-white person listed in the 1790 census who lived with Joseph Leach, but if one were to guess at the work in which this man engaged it would likely have been carpentry, painting, molding work, or other ship-building skills. Any of these trades would have required a desire on Joseph Leach's part to do some teaching and sharing of skills in the style of a guild craftsman.

Robert Miller Sr.

Born about 1704, in Salisbury Massachusetts, Robert Miller Sr. was named in the history books a mulatto. He may have been the son of Neb Miller, slave of Christopher Toppan of Hampton (see above). Ann Bolt is believed to have been his first wife. He married second Mehitable Stanyan, member of First Congregational Church of Hampton, and settled in Hampton Falls as early as 1738. Robert Sr. and Mehitable were almost immediately warned out of Hampton Falls. Whether from poverty or prejudice, the record does not say, but despite this shaky start, Robert Sr. did find work as a ship carpenter. Perhaps Robert knew Joseph Leach and his unnamed free, non-white householder. But once Robert Sr. became employed he was able to purchase his house which stood near then resident Samuel Cockburn. Robert was said to have been a man of great strength. His name disappears from the Hampton Falls tax roll in 1787. Robert Sr. died at age ninety-four in Fryeburg, Maine, just before the turn of the century.[10]

Robert Miller Sr. started a family tradition of military service in 1745 when he, along with about six hundred other New Hampshire men, was recruited to fight in the war with France. Miller served with Captain Edward Williams and saw action at the Siege of Louisburg on Cape Breton Island. The record shows that several men from Hampton Falls died of sickness and Robert Miller had "his arm shot off."[11] He later petitioned the New Hampshire Royal government for assistance because of his inability to work with one arm to support his large and growing family that included among others, John, Sarah, Ann, Dorothy, Jonathan, and Ebenezer.[12] Although he had enlisted in Massachusetts, since he was living in New Hampshire at the time of petition, he was denied any help from Massachusetts.

As happens sometimes in small towns, a neighbor of Robert's, Meshech Weare, made a claim in 1753, charging that Robert "had the carnal knowledge… at several times" of Katharine Bryan, "singlewoman," and "that she is now with child and that the said Robert did beget the same on her body."[13] Author Glen Knoblock surmises that this child was son, Robert Miller Jr., born about 1753.[14] However, it is possible that Neb Miller, Negro slave of Col Christopher Toppan, was not Robert Miller Sr.'s father but his son. It is notable that neither Neb nor Robert Jr. are names that show up in the probate records of Robert Sr. It is also possible that Robert and Katharine Bryan's child could be the unnamed free non-white person living with Joseph Leach in 1790, since both Robert and Joseph were ship carpenters in nearby communities.

Robert Miller Jr.

Robert Miller Jr. was born about 1753. Very little is known about his early life but he is believed to have married Betty Rollins about the time he enlisted from Kensington, New Hampshire, in 1775 in Captain Winthrop Rowe's company in Poor's 2nd New Hampshire regiment along with Jonathan, his brother. He describes himself as a farmer and is also described as "molatto." When he enlisted he had only a conditional acceptance to begin with. Later, the total count of men is recorded as, "total officers and rank and file 66 including the Molatto."[15] He received his payment in the form of a coat and enlisted again. He engaged in fighting in New York City, at Mount Independence, near Ticonderoga, and was finally discharged from active duty in 1780 after seeing action at Saratoga and Monmouth.[16] He ended up serving his country for five consecutive years. It is interesting to note that both the Miller and Burdoo families of free blacks have multi-generational lineages that are traceable because of their military service. In both cases, it is also the matriarchs, Dinah Small and Mehitable Stanyan, one woman African, the other white, who connect the families to the life of First Congregational Church in Hampton.

Jonathan Miller

Jonathan Miller, a free black or "mulatto."[17]

Jonathan, son of Robert Sr. and Mehitable and brother to Robert Jr., was born about 1755. He grew up on "Murray's row" in Hampton Falls. He took up his father's military tradition in 1775 when he enlisted with his brother, Robert, in Captain Winthrop Rowe's company in Col. Enoch Poor's 2nd New Hampshire regiment. He enlisted as a fisherman and was also paid his wages in blanket and coat money. He later enlisted and saw duty in the defense of Piscataqua Harbor. Jonathan fought at Fort Anne, New York, and in the Battle of Monmouth. In June of 1778, he reported as sick in the army hospital in Pennsylvania and in 1780 he is listed as having deserted—but more likely he was on furlough.[18]

While home on furlough, on April 20, 1781, Jonathan (and another man, named Eliphalet Rawlins) was charged by a James Man of Seabrook with having made a "violent assault" on him. Man said that they "chased him with clubs from said Hampton Falls to Seabrook and then and there threatened him in fear of his life or bodily hurt."[19] Although Jonathan pleaded not guilty, he was found "guilty of threatening the said James Man in a high handed manner whereby he appears to be in great fear and terror." Miller paid a fine and court costs in an amount of almost 109 pounds. He had land levied for a year and tasked with good and peaceful behavior. This was easy since Miller left town to finish his tour of duty.[20] When he returned home in 1780 he married another Rollins daughter, Rachel.

Throughout 1781 and 1782, Hampton Falls paid Jonathan for a few supplies. With six months left to serve, he hired

Joseph Green to fill out the remainder of his enlistment term. He asked Captain Isaac Frye to collect his remaining pay for him but ended up suing him for pay due. Jonathan won the suit in 1785 and then disappeared from Hampton Falls by 1790. His post-military life is a mystery, for the most part.[21]

Caesar Macling or McLain

Caesar served a very short term in the Revolutionary War from Hampton. He saw action at Winter Hill, outside Boston in 1775. Caesar is believed to have been owned by Rev. John Wilson, pastor of the Presbyterian Church in Chester, New Hampshire, who ministered there for forty-five years. Rev. Wilson was born in Ireland in 1709 and emigrated when he was just twenty years old to America. It is not known when Rev. Wilson acquired Caesar as a slave.[22]

The census of the town of Chester in 1753 lists one male slave, but no name is given. In 1775 in Chester, the census records three slaves as residents. Usually, a slave would enlist from the town where his owner lived. Oddly enough, Caesar McLain, in 1776, enlists to fight in the Revolutionary War from the town of Hampton. It was not unusual for a town to try to meet its quota of recruited soldiers by bartering with other nearby towns to "borrow" one of their soldiers to fulfill their quota. Perhaps this was the case for Caesar. His name also appears on a town census list from Portsmouth, dated 1777, with two other "Negro" men. One wonders if these were the other two slaves mentioned, along with Caesar, in the 1775 Chester census. Not much else is known about Caesar, but after the war, he does appear in the 1790 New Hampshire Census as a free, "non-white head of household" in Hampstead, New Hampshire, with one other person, likely his wife.[23]

Caesar (Brown)

Caesar, Abigail Brown's Negro man, granted his freedom 1751/2.

In the inventory of Hampton Falls, it states that Abigail Brown gives her Negro man, Caesar, his freedom by March 14, 1751/2:

> To all people to whom these presents may come, know ye that I, Abigail Brown, widow of John Brown late of Hampton Falls deceased, in the province of New Hampshire in New England. Know ye that I do by these presents do for me and my heirs, executor, administrators, and assigns, every one of us, clearly and absolutely promise, release, and forever quit you the said negro man Caesar from me and my heirs forever, after the service of four years, which four years will be ended on the fourteenth day of March and in the year 1751 and 2 and in confirmation of what is above written, I have hereunto set my hand and seal, this ninth day of May in the twenty first year of the reign of King George the Second. (Signed, sealed and delivered in presence of us. Jacob Brown and Jeremiah Pearson.[24]

It appears that in 1756/7, Caesar, was rated a free man in the town of Hampton Falls and Abigail's promise came true in the words of Warren Brown's history when he writes, "It was she who gave a Negro man, 'Caesar' his freedom in 1757."[25] It may be that Caesar even owned land in Hampton Falls, as his taxes were enough to indicate that this might be true. Warren Brown also imagined that Caesar moved to Pittsfield, New Hampshire, after receiving his freedom, but there is no record of his residence.

Long before Caesar gained his freedom, Hampton-born

Edmund Johnson, son of Peter Johnson and Ruth Moulton, married Abigail, daughter of Abraham Green. Edmund's father, Peter, was baptized in the Hampton church by Rev. Stephen Bachiler in 1639 and met an untimely death by drowning in the Hampton River in 1674. He was a prominent Quaker. His son, Edmund, was also a Quaker. He and Abigail Green had nine children whom they raised on the Hogpen Farm, now in Kensington. Edmund was rated there in 1709 but disappears from Kensington records before 1727. Edmund died in 1747, but not before his daughter, Abigail, married John Brown, son of Benjamin in 1715.

Who was this freedom-granting woman, Abigail Brown? Abigail was a Quaker like her father, Edmund, and her grandfather, Peter. It is also clear from Warren Brown's history, that it was Abigail who drafted the written codicil that traced the path to freedom for Caesar. It is rare in the stories of Hampton-area slaves for the female in the family to be the one who freed a slave owned by the family. One wonders if this particular story unfolds as it does because of events occurring in the community of the Society of Friends at the time Abigail freed Caesar.

Edmund Johnson, Abigail Brown's father, would have been five years old when, in 1676, Quaker William Edmondson at Newport, Rhode Island, wrote an anti-slavery letter of advice to the Society of Friends. As Abigail's children were growing up, in 1733, Elihu Coleman would have released his tract entitled *A Testimony Against That Anti-Christian Practice of Making Slaves of Men*. Around the time that Abigail was writing the words down on paper that would secure Caesar's freedom, Quaker John Woolman published the anti-slavery treatise *Considerations on Keeping Negroes,* and in 1758 Pennsylvania Quakers voted to cease buying and selling slaves altogether.

The rarity of a woman in a slave-owning household to be the person who declared the freedom of any slave, also may give us an insight into the character of Abigail Brown and her desire to grant justice to Caesar. In some cases, white, male slave owners thought of their wives as pure but mentally inferior to themselves. When a woman married, it was more often the case that any property or possessions that she might own became her husband's, including her slave. Since John died in 1747 and Abigail's codicil states that Caesar would be free "four years hence," in 1751/2, it must have been that her wishes regarding Caesar's fate were declared in the year her husband, John, died. We may never know if John asked her to set Caesar free before he died or whether it was entirely Abigail's idea. But in the patriarchal society of Abigail's day, often even the slave knew that the mistress's authority derived from her husband.

The clarity of Abigail's words invite one to imagine that it was some measure of genuine affection between Abigail and Caesar that prompted her action; especially if he had been a house servant, working in close proximity to her and her children. She may have wanted to do her best to make his life more bearable by the written guarantee of his freedom in the same way she wished her own children their best possible futures. Abigail's strength of purpose also gives the impression of a woman whose ideas about equality for all persons had taken shape in her heart and mind well before the ideas of equality for all people had begun to crystallize into a "call to arms" against Great Britain. One wonders if Caesar carried a copy of Abigail's words with him as he made his way toward Pittsfield. One hopes Caesar also carried a measure of her pluck.

Abigail died in 1753, shortly after Caesar was granted his freedom. In the years that followed her death, Benjamin Brown, Abigail's brother-in-law, married Sarah Gove and lived in South Hampton. Benjamin and Sarah Gove had a son whom they named Benjamin. He was known as Deacon Benjamin Brown and married Abigail Longfellow. In the 1790 Rockingham

County, New Hampshire, census of non-white families, Deacon Benjamin Brown, of South Hampton is listed as having one free non-white member residing with him. There is no mention by name of the free, non-white person residing with Deacon Benjamin. However, if Abigail freed Caesar close to the age of twenty-one, it is possible that Caesar, if he ran into financial difficulties in Pittsfield as many freed slaves did, may have decided to come back to the Brown family to see if any of Abigail's descendants would be willing to grant him shelter. If this were so, he may have come poor in material possession but rich in the dignity of his status as "free man."

So, the historical record is clear. By 1775 and during the run-up to the Revolutionary War, blacks, both freed and slave, became soldiers and sailors who fought on behalf of Hampton or her break-away towns. Some enlisted; others were "drafted" by their owners to meet a town quota. But, in the end, their contribution to the colonies' independence was enormous both in the success of the various small conflicts as well as the larger campaigns that occurred during the mid-eighteenth century. Hampton and every single daughter or granddaughter town saw enlistments of black men. Sometimes two generations, such as the Millers from Hampton Falls, the Burdoos from Lexington, the Twilights from Sandown and Vermont, and others enlisted and served with honor in some of the most violent battles.

What was different, however, was the reality of life for black soldiers and sailors after the war was over. Many slaves were granted their freedom following the end of the Revolutionary War, just as white soldiers were celebrating their freedom from England. But far fewer blacks came home from the war as landholders or men who could go back to running a business or farm. Other black soldiers or their spouses spent years of continual pleading and justifying their right to a government pension. The consequence of their freedom was poverty, a nomadic existence as they were warned out of one town after another as vagrants or the much less desirable choice of returning to their master's homestead and asking to "stay on."

CHAPTER 8
....

Did the Clergy of First Congregational Church Own Slaves?

A S PURITANS IN AMERICA are famously known for fleeing repressive systems of religious belief, it seems incongruous to discover just how many Puritan families headed by clergymen seemed untroubled by the owning of another human being. It certainly was the case that several of Hampton's early ministers included a slave or servant as part of the household. If no public record existed of a moment in an African American's life such as a baptism, marriage, or church membership, the other places one might discover their existence are through probate records, county pauper lists, occasional advertisements for runaways, or snippets of deed histories.

Chronology of Pastors

Rev. Stephen Bachiler (1638–1641), First Pastor

Because we have no probated will for Rev. Stephen Bachiler that lists his possessions and details to whom he may have left them, we might conclude that Stephen, himself, did not own an African-origin slave. But absence of evidence of a will leaves his slave-owning status inconclusive.

Rev. Timothy Dalton (1639–1661), Second Pastor

Rev. Timothy Dalton, who was called as a teacher to work with Rev. Stephen Bachiler, was an elderly man when he came to Hampton. He and his wife had no children and there is no record of him owning slaves during his years of service to the Church. His brother, Philemon Dalton, was a weaver and became a very prominent merchant in his day. The great-great-grandson of Philemon, Tristam Dalton, was not only a successful merchant, but also quite a statesman. In 1720, his father, Michael Dalton, built a grand mansion in Newburyport that was at the center of social events of the day. Originally the property included fine stables and gardens. With a wide colonial porch, Corinthian columns, and intricate carvings, (probably worked on by one or more of the woodworkers who also carved the ornamentation on some of the sailing vessels owned by the Daltons), the house itself contained twenty-five rooms. It was said that even these twenty-five rooms were scarcely enough to hold the Dalton family and their many guests and servants. Many of these servants were slaves who kept this large household running smoothly. One such slave is buried on Burying Hill in Newburyport, and on the headstone is carved, "**Faithful Pompey**."[1] Another slave, **Fortune**, married **Flora Taylor** in 1797 and together they had a son, **Primus**, who died in 1802 just before his father died in 1804. Rev. Timothy might well have been surprised at both the luxury of his descendants' living quarters as well the number of slaves they owned, for he owned none.

Rev. John Wheelwright (1647–1656), Third Pastor

Rev. Wheelwright, born in Saleby, England, arrived in Boston, Massachusetts, as a "non-conforming Puritan" with his second wife and five children in 1636. He served first a parish in what is now Quincy, Massachusetts, and was a follower of some of the freer thinking embraced by Ann Hutchinson, wife of William Hutchinson, Mrs. Wheelwright's brother. This thinking was condemned as seditious and contemptible by the Massachusetts General Court, and Rev. Wheelwright was banished from the church and the colony. He made his way up the Piscataqua River and the following spring he secured release from the Indians of rights to the land now known as Exeter, New Hampshire. The first year was difficult for the settlers, but since this was meant to be an ecclesiastical settlement, the church claimed 1638 as its founding year while the town claimed 1639 as its year of governmental organization. While at Exeter, Rev. Wheelwright is said to have owned an indentured servant as a housemaid, one Elizabeth Evans of Wales, but there is no record of him owning any African American slaves.

In the next generation of Wheelwrights, one of Rev. John's sons, Judge Samuel Wheelright, allowed in his will of 1700 this item: "I do give and bequeath unto Esther, my beloved wife, all my cattle of all sorts, with one negro servant named **Titus**."[2] Also in the will of Colonel John Wheelright, of Wells, who is Judge Samuel's son, there is included a mention of what this worthy member of the Christian church, who died in 1745, bequeathed to his wife: "In consideration of the love and affection I bear to my beloved wife, I give her all my cattle, and creatures of all kinds, **negro** or **molatto servants**."[3]

Later, in 1752, a great-great-grandson of Rev. Wheelwright's, Jeremiah, who was a successful cooper in Portsmouth, is said to have ordered two slaves from Barbados, a man and a woman. They were delivered by ship's master Archibald Smith of Somersworth, who traded out of Portsmouth where Jeremiah and his wife, Demaris, lived. When the slaves arrived, their health was so poor that they were unable to work in any productive way. Jeremiah sued the shipmaster for damages.

Cato, a black mariner, was purchased by Jeremiah on one of his voyages to Barbados. **Cato** lived with two other slaves, **Nero** and **Jane**, in the Wheelwright home at what is now Strawberry Bank, Portsmouth. In Jeremiah's will of 1768, he leaves Nero and **Jane** to Dr. Hall Jackson, for the sole use of Dr. Jackson's daughter, Mary Cram.[4] What becomes of **Cato** is not known.

Rev. Seaborn Cotton (1657–1686), Fourth Pastor

There is little recorded about Rev. Seaborn Cotton's life as pastor of First Congregational Church in Hampton. Rev. Seaborn did keep a commonplace book for several years during the time he served the church, which the New England Historic Genealogical Society possesses. In it, he wrote down quite a number of his favorite songs, prose, and certain ballads. During his years as pastor, he also included several family entries such as the dates of all of his children's births. In all these entries, however, there is none that indicates that Rev. Cotton owned a slave.

Rev. John Cotton (1687–1710), Fifth Pastor

Rev. John Cotton, son of Seaborn Cotton, was known to have inherited his father's commonplace book and to have recorded some of the early names of church members. When he began at Hampton, Rev. John had a very small congregation, but by his sudden death in 1710, he had added about two hundred members. None of the names of these members includes a notation of whether or not they were African American. There is also no ready evidence left in his own hand to indicate that he owned a slave.

Rev. Nathaniel Gookin II (1710–1734), Sixth Pastor

Rev. Nathaniel Gookin II was ordained to the First Congregational Church in November of 1710. He became the sixth pastor of First Congregational Church of Hampton, just as his father, Nathaniel, before him, had been the sixth pastor at Cambridge.

The great earthquake of 1727 occurred during Rev. Gookin's ministry and he delivered, only a few hours prior to the quake, a sermon which included these words of text, "The day of trouble is near." In this sermon he warns that something terrible is about to happen. In the evening came the violent shaking that threw the townspeople into great fear. Afterward, recalling the sermon, many believed he was possessed of the gift of divine knowledge, and, he soon became commonly known as "The Prophet." This extraordinary event not only garnered a title for Rev. Gookin, but it brought in a flurry of new members who believed that the world was coming to its end and that it was better to leave this life with a saved soul than not. The governor of the province was known to have declared on making the acquaintance of Rev. Gookin that "he had never met a man of such extraordinary dignity."[5] When Rev. Gookin II died, his gravestone is engraved with these words:

> Here lyes interred the body of the Revd Nathaniel Gookin MA & late pastor of the 1st Church of Christ Hampton who died Aug 25 DXXXIV in the 48th year of his age & the 27th of his ministry. He was a judicious divine; A celebrated preacher A most vigilant & faithful pastor; A bright ornament of learning and religion An excellent pattern of piety, charity & hospitality."[6]

Although there is no record of slave ownership by Rev. Nathaniel Gookin II, he and his wife, Dorothy Cotton, gave birth to several children. The stories of two of their children, Rev. Nathaniel Gookin [III], ordained to the North Hampton church in 1739, and his sister, Hannah, who married Patrick Tracy, follow as do the records of their slaves.

This brief look at potential slave-owning practices among the first six clergymen of First Congregational Church is exemplary of the larger socio-economic reality of Hampton. It is also consistent with the trends across the New England colonies. From the founding of the Hampton church and town in 1638 until the late seventeenth century, the written record of clergy owning slaves was sparse to non-existent. In fact, Shirk's inquest in 1671/72 remains the earliest story of slave-owning in Hampton of which there is a record. In the above instances, it is evident that it was not until early in the eighteen century that descendants of Hampton's clergy, and the clergy themselves, began to own slaves. In the brief catalogue of other Hampton clergy that follows, the reader will notice the trend toward slave-owning begin, even among the clergy of First Congregational Church and their descendants. It begins with Rev. Ward Cotton's slave, Jenny, whom he may have owned for twenty years while pastor of the church; he the one pastor, most careful to always make note of the race of owned persons in his record-keeping.

Rev. Ward Cotton (1734–1765), Seventh Pastor

"Jenny, [born about 1711], a Negro girl of Ward and Joanna Cotton" [baptized June 7, 1741.] "Jenny my Negro Woman aged about 40 of wind cholick" [died April 5, 1751].[7]

Jenny is the first "Negro servant" belonging to a Hampton pastor whose name is listed in one of the church's record books. Rev. Ward Cotton was seventh pastor of Hampton Church. He was the son of Rowland and graduated Harvard College in 1729. He was ordained in 1734 and not dismissed from First Congregational Church until 1765. Rev. Cotton married Joanna Rand about 1734, daughter of William Rand and Sarah Cotta. It is not certain whether Jenny came into the Cotton family through

Ward or Joanna. Rev Ward Cotton died in 1768. After Ward's death, Joanna married second Jonathan Gilman of Exeter.

Elizabeth Cotton, who was a daughter of Ward and Joanna, married Dr. Ebenezer Fisk in 1751 and removed to Epping. They owned a slave named Cato Fisk, whom they later freed. Cato settled in Exeter, but he struggled financially. On several occasions, Cato Fisk was warned out of various towns, Exeter (in 1787), Raymond (1796), Poplin (Danville, 1799), and Deerfield (1801). In 1799 and in 1801, his warning out included Ebenezer, Elizabeth, James, John, and Nancy, who were likely his family members.[8] Cato died in Epsom in 1824.

Rev. Ebenezer Thayer (1776–1792), Eighth Pastor

Rev. Ebenezer Thayer came to Hampton as one of three potential candidates for ministry, each of whom had been put forward by a small faction of the church body. The church record indicates that Rev. Ward Cotton had experienced a difficult leaving. The record is less than transparent regarding the justification for his dismissal—indicating vaguely his state of mind and moral character. An ongoing lawsuit regarding the exact boundaries of the parsonage, which overlapped in two towns, was nearing resolution and with Jeremy Belknap and John Marsh vying as candidates for the same pulpit with Rev. Thayer, a difficult choice needed to be made.

With discontent among the ranks of some, Rev. Thayer was installed, and although the record is silent on whether he owned slaves, we do know that he was tutor for a time to Dinah Chase prior to her joining the church. It is also true that his tenure saw the deaths of Caesar; Negro of Capt. Jeremiah Marston; an infant of Cesar Long's; Cesar Small; and Caesar Clough. To this day, none of their gravesites have been found.

Among all these deaths, Dinah Small and Philip Burdoo were married in 1783. This was the only marriage among so much death in this minority population among the worshipping congregation.

When a clergyman like Rev. Ebenezer Thayer performed marriages for freed slaves in the late 1700s, did he finally use the entire wedding ceremony? Did they say, "What God has joined together, let no man put asunder" because as freed blacks their union could now be secure and not torn apart based on the master's whim? Could a freed husband and wife actually begin to experience a marriage in which land or material possessions might be owned by both of them?

Could Rev. Thayer encourage the husband and wife to pledge their love until "death shall part us" and not wonder that this ancient religious rite was something altogether new for African-origin slaves who previously had been prevented from such sacred unions? Did Ebenezer wonder what it would be like for a black man to be able to support a family relying solely on his own physical labor? How long might it have taken a couple like Dinah and Philip Burdoo to rest secure in the knowledge that today, tomorrow, and the day after that, they could live inviolate as a family and their children would still call them and only them mamma and papa?

Throughout Rev. Thayer's pastorate it is fair to say that both the number of slave owners and the number of slaves had already begun to decrease. The Indian wars and the Revolutionary War took their toll on men and their families of every race. Unfortunately, the church record, while recording the deaths of African Americans, is silent on whether clergymen presided over their burials and, if so, where the majority of African Americans are buried in Hampton. It is fair to assume that clergy did preside and it is also fair to surmise that the spaces where the African Americans were buried were in the backs or corners of village and town cemeteries, along with other strangers or paupers in sites bereft of markers or tombstones.

Rev. Thayer's ministry extended through the whole of the Revolution and of the Confederation that preceded the adoption of the Constitution. He would have been a witness to both the country's struggle for freedom and liberty as well as the struggles of African men and women he had come to know personally as they began to take up lives as free, non-white heads of households. In the list of those Caucasians married by Rev. Thayer, nearly every woman's name is preceded by the title, "Miss" and every man's by "Mr." When he lists the marriage of the only African origin couple that he married, Dinah and Philip Burdoo, there is no title given for either person. He simply states their names and the date of their union. While this may be interpreted as a conscious or unconscious slight to their personhood, I would like to imagine him wishing them well even as he may have wished Dinah Chase, whom he tutored prior to her marriage to Prince Whipple. They, like all newly married couples needed every blessing possible.

Rev. Jesse Appleton (1796–1807), Ninth Pastor

The record is also silent regarding whether Rev. Appleton owned slaves during his tenure in Hampton. It is doubtful, as the attitudes regarding ownership of slaves had changed considerably. One of Rev. Appleton's daughters, Jane Means Appleton, grew up with considerably more education than most women of her day since her father left Hampton to become President of Bowdoin College. She was encouraged by her father to study and to share her opinions on the main topics facing the nation. Later, she married President Franklin Pierce and became First Lady of the newly organizing nation.

In the First Congregational Church Record Book, there is a special note written by Rev. Josiah Webster, which was discussed during a church session on June 9, 1811. This note dismisses President Appleton and his wife from the membership because of his call to become President of Bowdoin College and wishes them grace, mercy and peace. How interesting that Jane had a President for a father and for a husband!

Having more of an abolitionist background than her husband, it was Jane Appleton Pierce who persuaded President Pierce to release Dr. Charles Robinson, an ardent abolitionist and Republican, from a Kansas prison where he had been detained. Pierce, known for his kindness of heart, did so both for Jane and for the distraught wife of Dr. Robinson. Later, during the Civil War, the Pierces were divided on the opinion of ending slavery. Jane was for the ending of slavery immediately (if by war, then let it be so). President Pierce was for the constitution and the preservation of the union first and the abolition of slavery second.

Rev. Josiah Webster (1808–1837), Tenth Pastor

Rev. Josiah Webster began his tenure as pastor of First Congregational Church of Hampton in 1808 after having served in Essex (Ipswich), Massachusetts. In 1799, he married Elizabeth Knight, but his first child was not born until 1802. By the time that Elizabeth reached Hampton with Josiah to begin his pastorate, she would have been thirty-seven years old with three children and pregnant again by 1809. It may have been that Washington Cilley, listed below, became their servant in Hampton in order to help with the running of the household, especially given that Josiah led an active life as pastor and they eventually had seven children:

> "Washington Cilley, servant in ye family of Josiah Webster, aged 13 years, 10 mos. died of fever" [May 15, 1811].[9]

There is little known about Washington Cilley except the record of his death and the fact that he was a servant in Rev. Josiah

Webster's family. It is possible that Washington was not African American although his name was a name commonly given to African-American slaves. He may have been an indentured child or an orphaned child taken in by the pastor's family. Many slaves had been freed by the late 1700s, but we still cannot know with certainty if Washington was free or not.

However, if Washington was African American, he may have come into the Hampton network of slave holding families by way of Captain Joseph Cilley, and was perhaps even related to Lettice and Zene, the captain's slaves. There were generations of Cilleys who resided in both Hampton and Deerfield— some held slaves and others held voice against slavery. Captain Joseph was the son of sea captain, Thomas Cilley, and his wife, Ann Stanyan. Ann Stanyan was the granddaughter of Anthony Stanyan, a glover, born in 1611, who came to New England in a ship named *The Planter* and settled on "the Hill" in Hampton Falls.[10] Ann's brother-in-law, Theophilus Smith, was a slave owner, as was her son, Captain Joseph. But there has been no record found of her husband, Thomas, owning slaves.

Captain Joseph Cilley married Alice Rawlins and they had several children. When he died in 1775, Captain Cilley bequeathed to his wife a Negro woman, Lettice, and Negro man, Zene.[11] In a letter Alice wrote to her friend, Dorothy Jane, three years after Joseph's death, she said, "I am living with Abigail, now. It is very nice but I do miss Joseph, so. He was always so loving and thoughtful. He made a wonderful will – forgetting no one and arranging everything for my comfort. Our Negro slave, Lettice, is to stay with me while Boni stays with Joseph, my son."

This son, General Joseph Cilley, was the first son of Captain Joseph Cilley. He married Sarah Longfellow. Sarah and General Joseph Cilley lived first as residents of Deerfield, New Hampshire, and were given land which Sarah's father, Jonathan

Longfellow of Hampton Falls, had "bought" from Mr. Leavitt of Exeter in exchange for several slaves. Some of Jonathan's several slaves "came directly from the wilds of Africa."[12] Not all of the slaves Mr. Longfellow owned, however, were exchanged in the land deal. His son-in-law, General Joseph, and daughter Sarah got some of the Longfellow slaves. His other son-in-law, Nathaniel Batchelder, also received some of the slaves through his wife, Mary, sister to Sarah Longfellow Cilley.

In the 1790 Census of New Hampshire families with non-white members, it states that General Joseph Cilley still owned four slaves. Among them were Pompey, Chloe Cutler, and Lucy Light. Boni, mentioned in Alice's letter to Dorothy Jane, may have been the fourth slave. Another Cutler slave lived nearby, named Rufus Cutler. Rufus was the son of Tobias Cutler (slave of Colonel Enoch Hale of Rindge) and Dolly Pauls. Rufus married Diana Cilley of Deerfield, on March 12, 1823.[13] It is uncertain if Rufus Cutler's wife, Diana Cilley, was in any way related to the other Cilleys mentioned above, who are from Hampton and Deerfield.

Nathaniel Batchelder, born in 1732, was the three times great-grandson of Rev. Stephen Bachiler, first pastor of the Hampton congregation. Nathaniel married Mary Longfellow, niece of General Joseph Longfellow and sister to Sarah (Sally) Longfellow, wife of General Joseph Cilley. Both men, Joseph and Nathaniel, were officers in the Revolutionary War, serving from New Hampshire, and both were early settlers of Deerfield. About 1765, Simon Marston bought the Deerfield farm of Jonathan Longfellow, father-in-law of Nathaniel. Mr. Marston went away after that to Nova Scotia for a time before settling in Machias, Maine. As stated earlier, Mr. Longfellow is said to have paid for the farm with slaves and given some to his daughter, Sarah Cilley, and others to his daughter, Mary Batchelder, wife of Nathaniel. This is the first record of Nathaniel owning slaves.

Simon Marston's relatives owned the Deerfield farm for quite a while and according to records they left concerning the farm, "they kept as a choice historical relic an iron ring which was fastened to a post in the garrison, to which it is said Mr. Longfellow was accustomed to tie his slaves when it was necessary to punish them."[14] Mr. Marston is said to have taken this ring and fastened it to a post in his barn when he tore down the garrison that Longfellow had built. One would hope that the ring was used as a reminder that such punishment should never again be commonplace in any community that is meant to honor the rights and value of all persons.

With the mention of Washington Cilley, servant in Rev. Josiah Webster's family, we have come to the end of the clergy, slave-owning era in Hampton. There is not any further mention of slave-holding in the records of later ministers who served at First Congregational Church. Neither are there records which specifically speak of African slaves or servants in the records except to record a death. However, as members of the Hampton faith community made choices to found new churches in surrounding areas, the intermingled stories of their lives and the lives of their slaves continued.

North Hampton Congregational Church

Rev. Nathaniel Gookin III (1739-1766) North Hampton Congregational Church

Nathaniel Gookin III became the pastor of the North Hampton Congregational Church, one of First Congregational Church's daughter churches, shortly after his ordination. He married Judith, daughter of Captain Eliphalet Coffin of Exeter. In probate records for Eliphalet Coffin (1734/5) Eliphalet says:

> I give to my beloved wife Judith Coffin all my moveable estate within doors and without and my

Mulatto girl named Jinne and my Negro girl named Peg and all my stock of cattle and swine to be for her own use and at her dispose…and my Negro man, Jack, as long as she remains my widow…I give to my son, Peter Coffin, my Negro man, Jack after his mother is done with him."[15]

Peter Coffin, Eliphalet's son, married Dorothy Gookin, Nathaniel Gookin's sister. As the text of Eliphalet Coffin's probate record indicates, the Coffin family had several slaves, but it is uncertain whether Nathaniel Gookin and Judith Coffin Gookin or Peter Coffin and Dorothy Gookin Coffin received any of these slaves into their homes.

Nathaniel Gookin married second, Ann Fitch and third, Love Wingate. He died in 1766. In an excerpt by Charles E. L. Wingate concerning the life and letters of Paine Wingate, (Love's nephew), a preacher, farmer, and statesman, he states, "When Paine was a little over nine years old [1748]; he had the pleasure of attending the first wedding in the family since his birth. It was a fortnight before thanksgiving when Love Wingate, the ninth child of the elder Paine, was married in the Amesbury Church to Rev. Nathaniel Gookin of North Hampton."[16] Paine was said to have remembered there being slaves in the household of his grandfather, Joshua Wingate. Records mention in 1752, Dinah (see above under Dinah Chase Whipple) and in 1779, "Peter, servant of John Wingate." Nathaniel would perhaps have known Dinah Chase Whipple or known of her through Love, but not likely Peter, whose name occurs in the records long after Nathaniel's death in 1766.

Hannah Gookin, another of Nathaniel's sisters, was born in 1724. She married Patrick Tracy, born in Ireland. He came to Newbury, Massachusetts, as a poor youth, worked hard and soon became a ship owner and dealer in West Indian goods—one of the town's wealthiest merchants. He kept attorney John Lowell busy with a significant amount of legal work. In 1773, Lowell took on the case of Caesar Hendrick, "a colored man." It was the first case of its kind that involved a black man suing his owner, in this case, Richard Greenleaf of Newbury, for holding him in bondage as a slave. Richard Greenleaf was a ship builder and husband of Marcia Toppan, daughter of Caleb Toppan. Caleb Toppan is believed to have been the builder of the Leavitt barn housed at Tuck Green near the Tuck Museum, in Hampton.

Joshua Coffin, in his history of Newbury tells it this way, "October 10, 1773 Extract of a letter from Newburyport...we have lately had our court week when the novel case of Caesar Hendrick against his master in an action of £50 lawful money damages plaintiff £18 damages and cost."[17]

The decision in the case awarded Caesar his freedom and caused quite a stir in the community. Efforts intensified, with attorney John Lowell leading the way toward ending the practice of slavery. Jonathan Jackson, Lowell's friend and fellow lawyer, owned a slave named, "Pomp" among others. After the verdict in Mr. Hendrick's case, Jonathan released Pomp for a fee of five shillings. Pomp went on to enlist in Continental service in 1776 and became a fifer. Taking his cue from Mr. Jackson, Patrick Tracy, who also owned slaves, freed "his faithful black man, Apropos, and his wife." Both had lived a long time in Tracy's family and were trusted and well-respected in the town of Newburyport. In his will, Mr. Tracy made provisions for a home and life-time income for these two. He specified that they could improve the gardens and in the will he declares that he expects his children to continue their support for Apropos and his wife, especially into their old age, when they might become frail.[18]

It is without certain knowledge that I associate "Pomp Jackson," Jonathan Jackson's slave, with information about the paupers of Rockingham County, New Hampshire. It is certain that a great many freed slaves settled in Exeter following the Revolutionary War and many slipped into poverty, especially when freedom was not accompanied by land ownership. Constable Simon Ward was told to warn a Pomp Jackson to leave the town of North Hampton in January of 1794. Again in February of 1794, Pomp was warned out of Exeter by Constable Joseph Lamson.[19] Apparently Pomp didn't listen very well to the constable since the marriage records for Exeter show a Pomp Jackson marrying a Susanna Dimond in April of 1794. If this Pomp Jackson is, indeed, the same man freed by Attorney Jonathan Jackson, then it is difficult to realize that a freed slave able to reside anywhere, fared less well than Apropos and his wife, who although free, remained as gardeners in the home of their owner.

During the years between 1720 and 1790, when Hannah and Nathaniel Gookin's stories take place, we see a larger number of families able to own more than one slave. In Hampton this was true for Rachel Freese and Sarah Toppan. Slave-owning became more wide-spread, with the possibility of either husband or wife bringing to a marriage a slave bequeathed to them by a parent. Provisions were also being made toward freedom and care for newly-freed slaves beyond the lifetime of the slave owner. Evident, as well, is the fact that when this care was not given, those freed who lacked land or were no longer physically able to work, fared far less well. This pattern is very characteristic in the lives of freed slaves following service in the Revolutionary War.

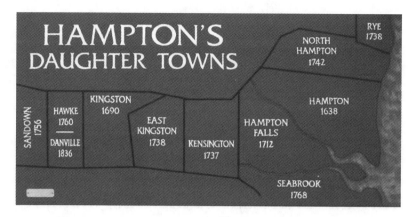

The Daughter and Grand-daughter Towns that are Hampton's Descendant Communities. Photo Courtesy of Hampton Historical Society's Tuck Museum, Hampton, NH.

CHAPTER 9
....

The Widening Circle:
African Americans of the Daughter and
Granddaughter Churches

T HE TOWNS OF HAMPTON, Exeter, Portsmouth, and Dover were established from 1643 to 1680, however, these communities were part of "Old Norfolk County," one of the four lands administrative districts created by the General Court, and administered by local leadership during the early years that followed the settlement of the Massachusetts Bay Colony. On the first day of the first month of 1680, the New Hampshire Royal Province was established, and Hampton became "Hampton, New Hampshire." Rev. Seaborn Cotton was pastor of the First Congregational Church at the time. In the First Congregational Church Record book, known today as Vol. I & II, John Cotton, Rev. Seaborn's son, has left a few fragments from the records kept by his father. Unfortunately, none of these records refers to the establishment of Hampton as a town in New Hampshire.

Beginning in 1694, during Rev. John Cotton's tenure as pastor, the town of Hampton began to be re-shaped as clusters of settlements, each about six miles distant from Hampton Center. Groups of Hampton church members began to petition the church and town for "dismissal" to form new settlements and new parishes.

The process of new town and new church settlements was an uneven one. These dismissals were not usually the consequence of theological discord. Rather, as the population grew and ventured inland, the long walk across the marsh to church became too much for a growing number of families, especially during the winter when the marsh was muddy. It simply made more sense to begin a "related" parish closer to home. Sometimes the dismissal resulted first in the establishment of a town, born of acreage once belonging to Hampton, and the incorporation of the parish happened shortly after. Kingston, for example, was established in 1694 but it wasn't until September 5, 1725, that a group of nine persons was dismissed from First Congregational Church of Hampton to form the Parish at Kingston. Of this group, there were six men and three women. At other times it was the parish that was born first. In either case, to be considered a daughter church of First Congregational Church, the dismissals had to involve the release of existent members of the "mother" church.

Other types of dismissals did occur. September 11, 1698, Rev. John Cotton dismissed thirteen members of First Congregational Church. These members were "dismissed in order to their being incorporated into a church state in Exeter." Ten of these thirteen members were women and they were dismissed so they might be incorporated into an already established church in an already established town. This practice was called giving someone a "letter of transfer" which enabled them to move from one Congregational Church to another. This dismissal to Exeter was not considered a daughter dismissal, whereas the Kingston Parish dismissal is determined to be a daughter dismissal. The three main daughter dismissals, considered as such by succeeding generations of church historians, were those to Kingston (1725),

North Hampton (petitions started in 1719 and were finalized in 1742), and Hampton Falls (petitioned 1712 and church founded in 1718).

Of these daughters, only North Hampton did not go on to produce a "granddaughter" parish. However, during the twenty-three years between the first petition of North Hampton for release from Hampton and the final agreement to release, 1800 acres belonging to North Hampton families were annexed to Rye, so some of that land may have provided the spot on which the Rye Congregational Church had its beginnings.

The Kingston settlement eventually spawned parishes in East Kingston (town set off in 1738 and parish established 1739 under Rev. Peter Coffin), Danville (or Hawke, 1760), and Sandown (10 dismissed in 1759 under Rev. Josiah Cotton). The Hampton Falls parish spawned a parish at Kensington (1734 under Rev. Jeremiah Fogg) and had a small hand in the Seabrook parish. The daughters are three and the grands are six if we include Rye and Seabrook. In every town except Sandown, a worshiping congregation still exists today who can trace their roots back to one of these dismissals.

The Presbyterian schism occurred in the First Congregational Church between 1792 and 1807. During this time, the Church gave up its role as the sole denomination represented in the town of Hampton. Thus, all of the dismissals that occurred prior to 1792 would have been considered new church starts and each congregation would have functioned in accord with Congregational polity. In many cases, the newly founded congregations were the only parish in the new town. Only after the Presbyterian schism did most Congregational churches establish Congregational Societies in order to discriminate between those who attended worship and those who became members of the Congregational Society, since by the mid-1800s the number of denominational choices had grown to include Methodists, Baptists, Presbyterians, and Quakers.

If one were to count the number of new church starts in the Congregational tradition in New Hampshire in the forty-year span between 1973 and 2013, one could count them on one hand with fingers left over, so changed is the landscape of and cultural need for congregational gatherings for the purpose of worship and mission. In fact, New Hampshire currently ranks last among the six New England states when counting the percentage of people attending worship weekly in a local congregational setting. Therefore, in this roughly forty-year span of time, between 1718 and 1760, to have nine new churches established gives evidence of the passion and sentiment of our founding fathers and mothers for not only the gospel's good news but for a place to gather for the preaching, teaching, and sharing of that good news.

Because of this active dismissal process, which began under Rev. Nathaniel Gookin and continued until the middle of Rev. Ward Cotton's pastorate, I have chosen to include some of the named slaves and their slave-owning families who resided in the various daughter and granddaughter churches of First Congregational Church. This seems to honor the contiguous movement of families as the generations were born over the course of the decades between 1710, when comprehensive record-keeping began, and 1792, the beginning of the Presbyterian schism. In moving from the records of Hampton slaves owned by Hampton residents to include slaves listed in the surrounding towns and parishes, not all the slaves listed in any given daughter or grand-daughter town may appear in this work. The focus is on those slaves linked primarily to families first discovered in the church and town records of Hampton. It will be the work of others to establish a more detailed record of those African Americans who were part of the new church starts and new town starts.

The African American Community of the Daughter Church of Hampton Falls

A small group of members who resided on the south side of the falls were the first of the Hampton Parish to ask for a dismissal. They were faithful attendees at worship, but a long stretch of salt marsh separated them from the Hampton meetinghouse and often at high tide the stretch of road flooded. By the time they reached Hampton their feet were frozen and the long hours sitting in a cold building with freezing feet were not conducive to focused attention to the sermon. The first move out to Hampton Falls involved the construction of a house for shelter and relief that was used also for worship on the Lord's Day. By 1701, this group had settled Rev. Theophilus Cotton as their first pastor. Theophilus was the nephew of Rev. Seaborn Cotton, the cousin of Rev. John Cotton, and the uncle of Rev. Ward Cotton, who were all pastors of First Congregational Church in Hampton.

Syppio or Sippai (Cotton), an American Indian servant or slave

It was ten years later, in December of 1711 that forty-nine members of the old Hampton church were dismissed in order to form the Hampton Falls Church—twenty-one males, thirty-five females, and at least one American Indian servant, Syppio (or Sippai). We know about this servant because of meticulous record-keeping by both Rev. Theophilus Cotton and later by Rev. Whipple. As Rev. Cotton declares, it was in 1713 that Syppio (or Sippai) his own Indian servant, was baptized by him, "as a means to engage to bring him up in the fear of God."[2]

Rev. Theophilus Cotton's wife, Mary Gookin Gedney Cotton, died without children in 1726. Just prior to her death, in 1725, "Theophilus Cotton of Hampton, deeded to Jonathan

Poore, of Newbury, "all that my Indian boy Sippai, aged about 16."[3] Rev. Cotton, himself, died shortly after Sippai was deeded.

Elizabeth Varrell

In 1729, Elizabeth Varrell was baptized. Rev. Joseph Whipple adds, "My wife and I engaged for her" but it is unclear whether he and his wife were sponsoring Elizabeth for baptism as an infant or an adult, and neither is it clear from this record if she was African American. However, if she were a young child and an African American, she may have been the mother of William Varrell, an African-American soldier from North Hampton. (See the North Hampton record for William's church relationship.)

Fortunatas, Pompey and Fortune (Whipple)

In 1733, Fortunatas, "my Negro boy,"[4] was baptized by Rev. Joseph Whipple. One may assume that Fortunatas was a young lad, but there is no other information about him to indicate where he was born, nor his age at baptism. As mentioned earlier, Rev. Whipple gave Fortunatas his freedom in 1755, a short time before Rev. Whipple died. Although Pompey and Fortune are listed in his diary as belonging to him, Rev. Whipple recorded nothing of their fates.

June or Jerro (Brown)

In 1734, June, Mr. J. Brown's "Negro man" was baptized and owned the covenant. Owning the covenant was the term used for joining one's self to the church. One of the oldest covenants still in existence, the Salem Church Covenant of 1629, states that the aspiring member agrees to "walke together in all his (God's) waies."

A second source looks like "Jerro, Mr. I. Brown's Negro man." It is difficult with only the initial *J* to know for certain whether June [or Jerro] belonged to John Brown Sr., who died in 1747 or John Brown Jr., his son, who died in 1745. John Brown Sr. was the son of Jacob Brown and inherited a large tract of land near the falls. Again, little other information is available, except by way of imagining that June or Jerro had tasks related to the care of that large tract of land.

Jane (Blake)

Also in 1734, Jane, Negro to Philemon Blake Sr. was baptized. The Blake family is connected to two of the slaves in this work: Philemon Blake Sr. owned Jane and Philemon Blake Jr. owned Jude Hall. No familial link was found between Jane and Jude Hall and it may be that they lived separately on each of the Blake properties. There is not a record of Jude Hall being baptized, but his story occurs in a later section.

Andrew (Worth) and Dinah (Worth)

Christopher Hussey's farm in Hampton Falls was one of the largest. After his death, his descendants stayed on the farm for a number of years until, soon after 1730, Joseph Worth came to live on the property after being dismissed from Dr. Coleman's Brattle Street Church in Boston. He was admitted to the Hampton Falls Church in 1736 and thereafter he became prominent in both church and town affairs as a deacon and selectman. In 1736, upon Joseph's joining the church, Rev. Whipple married both of Joseph's slaves, Andrew and Dinah, in the church.[5] Joseph Worth is listed as residing in Hampton Falls until about 1794, when he removed to Epsom. There is no further information about how long Andrew and Dinah remained in town—except to note that Joseph Worth does not appear in the census of 1790 as owning any slaves and his probated will does not contain any information about the transfer of slaves to any of his family members. Andrew and Dinah's marriage is the only one recorded in the Hampton Falls

Church in which two slaves were joined as one. Philip Burdoo and Dinah Small Burdoo were the one African couple married in the old Hampton church. What is interesting is that Andrew and Dinah were married in 1736 in a daughter church, while Dinah and Philip were married in the mother church in 1783, nearly fifty years later.

James (Weare)

In 1739, James, "Coll Wear's negro man" was baptized and owned the covenant.[6] Colonel Meshech Weare was a prominent leader in Hampton Falls having served in many and various positions. In 1738, Meshech married Elizabeth Shaw. She was the daughter of Samuel Shaw, who was deacon in both the Hampton and Hampton Falls churches. She was also great-granddaughter of Roger Shaw, who was one of five original farmers in Hampton Falls. When Meshech married Elizabeth he came into possession of the farm property owned by her father, Deacon Samuel, and most likely also came into the possession of James, "his Negro man." There is no mention of James in Meshech Weare's probated will.

Peggy (Demon) (Fifield) and Jupiter (Fifield)

Mr. Fifield's Negro man, Jupiter, was baptized and owned the covenant. I wonder if Jupiter, along with other slaves, would rather have agreed to walking in his own way with God and his neighbor as a free man when he "owned the covenant" in 1734?[7] Also listed as belonging to Mr. Fifield in the church records were Peggy, Fifield's "negro woman," and Rachel and Zilpah.

Zilpah, Daughter of Peggy (Demon) (Fifield) and Rachel, daughter of Jupiter (Fifield)

Rachel, daughter of Jupiter, Mr. Fifield's Negro man, was also baptized in 1741. In 1742, Peggy Demon (Dirnan), Fifield's

Negro woman, gained full Communion when she owned the covenant, and Zilpah, Peggy's daughter, was baptized.[8]

William Fifield was a prominent citizen of Hampton. Benjamin Fifield, his son, also an early settler, was ambushed by Indians on his way to church one Sabbath in 1706 and was killed. Since he was killed near a large rock, the farm nearby was later known as "Indian Rock Farm." Another young lad, who was believed to have been a relative, was carried off at the same time. Today that farm is still kept as a homestead and is in the southern part of Hampton Falls, first called Hampton.

Benjamin was about sixty years old at the time of this incident. He and Mary Colcord (his wife) had a son, Jonathan, born in 1685. Jonathan lived in Hampton Falls and married Hanna Wait. Jonathan is probably the Fifield who saw to it that Peggy and Zilpah, as well as Jupiter and Rachel, were baptized and owned the covenant, since he was, like his grandfather before him, a prominent citizen and church leader for many years. Jonathan and Mary had no children and one wonders what the relation was like between them and Rachel and Zilpah. Not enough is known about Rachel and Zilpah to know whether they were friends, step-sisters or perhaps two daughters of two unrelated slaves, Deacon Fifield's Negro man, Jupiter and Negro woman, Peggy. There is no mention of the Fifield slaves in Jonathan's 1771 will.

Caesar (Batchelder)

In 1742, Caesar, "Negro servant of J. Batchelder" was baptized and owned the covenant.[9]

There is scant information about Caesar. While it is not certain, Joseph Batchelder, born in 1698 in Hampton and lived in Hampton Falls, seems the most likely person to have owned Caesar.

Joseph and his wife, Mary, had several children who died of

throat distemper and Caesar may have been involved in helping to care for these children, perhaps even burying them.

Jack and Venus (Tilton)

In 1742, Jack, "negro Servant to Capt. Tilton" was baptized and owned the covenant.

Captain Jethro Tilton was born in 1684 in Hampton, son of Daniel and Mehitable (Sanborn) Tilton. Daniel, Jethro's father, was a prominent businessman in Hampton Falls. He owned quite a bit of land and built a blockhouse to fortify the town during the Indian wars. Both Daniel and Jethro, his son, were blacksmiths.

It is not out of the question to imagine that Jack, servant to Jethro, was a strong man. This would have been a necessity if he helped with shoeing animals with the iron shoes that Jethro fashioned at the forge. He would also have needed to wield a sledge hammer and split wood to keep the forge fueled.

When Captain Jethro died in 1754, his will did not include any mention of Jack. The will simply states: "Jethro gives to his wife his Negro woman named Venus."[10] Venus, however, is not listed in the church records as ever having been baptized or ever having owned the covenant as Jack did. There is also no record of Venus and Jack ever being married or even knowing one another.

Additional Tilton Slaves

Dinah and Judah Snelling

Captain Jethro Tilton's brother, Joseph, was born in 1677 in Hampton and married Margaret Sherburne. Joseph had a son, Jonathan, who was born in 1708 in Hampton and married Margaret Shaw. Jonathan, it appears, had servants and Indian servants (their actual ethnic status is not clear) living with him and worshiping with him. In 1749 Jonathan's servants Dinah Snelling and Judah Snelling were baptized and owned the covenant in the Hampton Falls church. It is not known if Dinah and Judah were married or if they were siblings. It is also not clear whether Dinah and Judah were African-origin slaves. However, an Asa Snelling is recorded as having served in the Revolutionary War as a black soldier, enlisting from his residence in Penobscot, Maine. While it is not confirmed, Asa may have been a realtive of Dinah and Judah Snelling of Hampton Falls.

Indian Slaves

Judith; Abigail Prince and Margaret

Also, in 1750, "Judith, daughter of Jonathan Tilton's Indian woman" [was baptized].[11] Though Judith is listed as having an Indian mother, there is no mention of her father. There were very few Indian slaves or servants among the records of any of the Hampton area towns, although Indian slaves were more common in other New England states. However, in 1741, two Indians, Abigail Prince and her daughter Margaret, were baptized in the First Congregational Church in Hampton.[12] Again, there is no mention of Margaret's father.

The African American Community of the Granddaughter Church at Kensington

At a church meeting on October 2, 1737, the congregation at Hampton voted to dismiss several persons "in order to their being embodied into a Church State in ye third parish of this Town" with "Mr. Jeremiah Fogg ye Pastor Elect, Edward Tuck and his wife, Edward Lock, Hannah Shaw, wife of Joseph, Widow Sarah Batcheller, and Abigail Cram, wife of Benjamin." This was attested by Rev. Ward Cotton.[13] The following month, the church voted five younger deacons to attend the ordination of Mr. Jeremiah Fogg, which they did. What this church account does not tell, however, is the story of Phyllis Parsons, who also went to Kensington with Rev. Jeremiah Fogg and his new wife, Elizabeth Parsons.

Phillis Parsons (Fogg) and the Mingo Brothers

Phillis's story begins in South Hampton, the town that abutted Kensington and it includes characters from Hampton, Epping, and Kensington.

William Mingo, believed to be a free black, born of Thomas and Lydia Tyre, was a "colored soldier who died on the frontier."[14] He died engaged to Phillis Parsons. Before he died, there may be another leaving in William's story revealed in a runaway ad in the *Boston Gazette*:

> Ran-away from his master Nathaniel Smith of Eppen, in the Province of New Hampshire, a Negro Man Servant named William Mingo, about 29 Years old, speaks good English, born in New-England, about 5 Feet 8 Inches high, something slim – Had on when he went away, a blue Homespun Coat, a blue Jacket without sleeves, Leather Breeches, light Worsted Stocking. Whoever takes up said Negro Servant, and will convey him to the Subscriber, shall have FIVE DOLLARS Reward, and all necessary Charges paid. All Masters of Vessels and others are hereby cautioned against harboring, concealing or carrying off said Servant on Penalty of the Law. Eppen, 23rd August 1767. NATHL SMITH[15]

Perhaps this suspected "free black" had decided that working for Nathaniel might provide him with a way to earn a living and had not bargained on just how much he had lost by living as a servant. Perhaps his running away was also his running toward enlisting as a soldier. Or this could be a different William Mingo altogether, from the William, born of Thomas and Lydia. For that William had two brothers, Ebenezer and Paul, and possibly a nearby uncle in Robert Mingo. Robert died in Haverhill, Massachusetts, of consumption in 1757. He was fifty-seven years old when he died "a free Negro," according to the death record. Of Paul's life we know only that he married Anna Summetsworth in 1773, but nothing else. So, we continue with Ebenezer Mingo's story and that of his plucky wife, Phillis, who committed themselves to freedom with all its joys and its costs.

South Hampton was incorporated in 1743. Prior to 1743, the land named South Hampton, had been part of Salisbury and part of Amesbury, Massachusetts. Records of the South Hampton Congregational Church indicate that only two pastors served the church. First, Rev. William Parsons served as minister from 1743 until 1762. He was succeeded by Rev. Nathaniel Noyes who was the second and last minister of the church, serving from 1763 until 1774. Rev. William Parsons was the son of Rev. Joseph Parsons and Elizabeth Thompson. Joseph and Elizabeth owned at least two slaves that we know of: Judith,[16] who died in 1729, and Phillis, who was to become the slave to Elizabeth Parsons, Rev. William's sister, and her new husband, Jeremiah Fogg.

On July 17, 1739, Parson Jeremiah Fogg married Elizabeth Parsons and brought her on a pillion behind him to the new manse in Kensington. Deacon Abraham Moulton accompanied them and carried behind him Phillis Parsons, a small black girl, who was Elizabeth's slave.[17] Apparently, Phillis was a bright and intelligent young woman and grew up to fall in love with William Mingo. When word was received of his death on the frontier, one wonders if Phillis had anyone who shared her loss and grief. Did she have parents living nearby or siblings?

The record does not answer such questions. However, when Rev. Joseph Parsons died, his probate inventory listed "1697 pounds 7 shillings; part of which was one negro woman, 90 pounds, and one negro man decrippled, 100 shillings."[18] This woman was not Phillis, since she had been with Elizabeth and Jeremiah Fogg for many years. It is possible that the "decrippled" man was Primus, a slave who lived with Rev. Fogg and his family after Rev. Parsons died. Although we don't know when Primus arrived at the Foggs, we know that Primus was known as a simple man, who lived well into his later years.

Sometime after 1739, well into her years of service to Elizabeth Fogg, Phillis became engaged to William Mingo's brother, Ebenezer. Phillis refused to be married, however, until she should be free. This was because the determination of whether an African-American child was free or not depended on the status of the mother's freedom. Phillis is believed to have said after William's death, "I refuse to be married [to Ebenezer] until I should be free, for I declare that I will never bring a slave into the world."[19]

In order to accomplish her freedom, Phillis left Kensington and went to Salisbury, in the province of Massachusetts, and lived a year and a day, probably keeping dark, (or remaining hidden indoors for most of that time).

Upon the first day she came out of hiding, in the course of strolling down the sidewalk, the town selectmen came to warn her out of town. They believed that she, as an African American woman living alone, would out of necessity become a ward of the town. Not wanting another "burden" on the town coffers, they asked her to move along. Phillis was said to have turned, made a polite courtesy and said, "Gentlemen, you are one day too late for by the laws of the time I have not only gained my freedom but also my status as a resident of Salisbury."[20] Phillis's days of serving Elizabeth Fogg as her slave were over.

Phillis Quash—not "Parsons," for this was her chosen name now that she was free—married Ebenezer Mingo in 1764. In 1768, Lidia was born, free-born daughter of Ebenezer and Phillis. And a year later, in 1769, Ebenezer Mingo and Phillis joined the church in South Hampton. Later, in 1769, Ebenezer and Lidia, children of Ebenezer and Phillis, were baptized. In 1774, Eli, another son, was baptized. Phillis is said to have taught school among the white people, saying very proudly, "It's no small thing to be brought up in a minister's family."[21]

Since many Puritan families saw it as their duty and commission to teach literacy and Christianity to their slaves, it is possible that Elizabeth and Jeremiah blessed Phillis's adventure toward freedom. If they knew of her hiding place, they may have even supported her in some discreet ways, possibly by teaching her to read and do her sums. They may have even given her a stipend to use during the time she spent in hiding. The record does not verify whether this is true, but hearts can hope that the Foggs would have done for Phillis and Ebenezer what they would have done for their own children, out of a sense of what is just.

In 1791, Lidia Mingo married Jess Smith, and in 1800, Eli Mingo and Violet Whittier were married. In 1798, Fanny Mingo and Simon Symonds were married, and in 1800, Charlotte Mingo married Joshua Brown in Newburyport.[22] It is unclear whether Charlotte and Fanny were also children of Ebenezer and Phillis.

The Mingos, like so many other post-Revolutionary War families, lived in some poverty and struggled to support their family. They may have gained their freedom, but of what use was freedom without money to purchase land and build a permanent home to grow food for your family? Gradually they sank into poverty. When they needed assistance from the town of Amesbury the town selectmen voted that they should "put out the one Nigar Boy for 25, 6d a week."[23] Members of the Mingo family were warned out of Kensington in 1774 and in 1780 were warned to depart Northwood.[24] After the warning out of Northwood, the Mingo family name appears in the 1790 Census of Amesbury, Massachusetts, which lists Ebenezer Mingo as head of a household containing four "non-white free persons."[25] When Phillis died in 1796, Ebenezer Mingo married Tryphena Sharp of Exeter. Ebenezer died in Salisbury, Massachusetts in 1807.

Jude Hall (Blake Jr. /Healey)

Jude Hall was born sometime between 1744 and 1755. He was the slave of Philemon Blake Jr of Kensington and was later sold to Nathaniel Healey.[26] Philemon Jr. was born in Hampton in 1705. He removed to Kensington where he was chosen as one of five provincial deputies sent to Exeter. It is surprising that Philemon found it necessary to sell Jude. Both farming and travel associated with political appointments were reasons for needing extra labor, and slaves were considered a good capital investment.

Jude apparently grew unhappy with Mr. Healey, his new owner, and soon ran away. He joined the army and became one of the longest-serving soldiers in the Revolutionary war. He was given his freedom and one hundred dollars for serving throughout the entire Revolution. It was said that he could "lift a barrel of cider and drink from the bunghole."[27] For this strength, he earned the nickname "Old Rock."

Apparently Jude was not involved as a baptized member of any church, either in Kensington or in Exeter, nor did he own the covenant of either church. Rather, his record is one of caring for his family and struggling to help his neighbors. After the war, it was difficult for blacks to make a living. Jude was warned out of Exeter in 1787.[28] He eventually moved back, however, where he married Rhoda Paul. They had ten children. It is said that for a time, the family lived in Exeter with Enoch Rowe. Later, Jude and his family were warned to depart from Stratham, and then in 1795, warned to depart Exeter again. In the end, the Hall family built a cabin in the woods near present-day Drinkwater Road. On his pension application, Jude made an inventory of his goods. The cabin is listed as having two rooms where he and Rhoda raised ten children! He also lists a shovel, some tongs, earthenware dishes and small pieces of furniture of little value. He was a fisherman and perhaps kept his family fed by this means, but one can easily imagine some meals with little more than fish on the plates that children took turns using.[29]

Jude was involved in several legal actions in his life. An 1801 writ, executed by Jude Hall against Jonathan Melcher, a white man, is significant. Jonathan Melcher was a descendant of Edward Melcher who had come to the area from Wales. The original Melcher farmstead abutted the Pike farmstead, the first over the line between Exeter and Hampton Falls, on its back boundary. The Melcher farmstead faced the present-day Drink-water Road, close to Jude Hall's homestead. Hall initiated "a plea of trespass" against Melcher because:

> [W]ith force & arms broke and entered the pl[an]t[iffs]s dwelling house in Exeter aforesaid & being so entered he, the D[efenden]t then & there with like force broke open an inner door in said house and totally ruined the same and by abusive and threatening language greatly alarmed & terrified the wife & children of the pl[an]t[iff].[30]

Justice Parker examined the case, and heard testimony by Jude, Jonathan Melcher, and even Jude's daughter, Dolly, who was interviewed as an eyewitness. There is no explanation given for Melcher's assault on Jude's house, nor is the final settlement of the case recorded. However, what is important is that as a free black person, Jude Hall had access to the court system to take legal action against a threat from his white neighbor.

Jude was also the chief government witness in the trial of John Blaisdell, who was alleged to have killed John Wadleigh. Jude was asked to the bench three times to testify and a part of that testimony is recorded thus:

> Between 8 and 9 on the evening of the 18th, somebody knocked at my door. My house is near the Exeter line and about a mile and a quarter from Folsom's. Told my children to open the door. Blaisdell came in and appeared frightened, and asked where the Captain was, (meaning me.) He said, he wanted me to help lead W[adleigh] in, that he was drunk and had been fighting with a sleigh. Blaisdell said that he would not have carried him into his (W.'s) own house for ten dollars, that he would have died if he had taken him up, and that he had led him from the Cove bridge. Wadleigh's house is between the Cove and mine, about 30 rods from mine. I heard heavy groans, found the deceased, lying on his side. I lifted Wadleigh up and led him home—he appeared to shudder with cold. I got a fire which he seemed to need. Blaisdell offered to take his hat—he drew back—then his handkercheif he still drew back—he next offered him a chair but he stood stiff. Blaisdell went to take Wadleigh's hat and Wadleigh shewed [sic] great horror whenever Blaisdell came near him— after about five to ten minutes Blaisdell went away and wanted me to go home with him—I said don't go, and Blaisdell said he must go to take care of his cattle—Wadleigh died about three quarters of an

hour before day—I was with him at that time—Blaisdell's house is in Kensington about a half a mile from
my house.[31]

John Blaisdell was a nearby neighbor to Jude. Blaisdell and
Wadleigh seem to have worked together from what Jude later
explains about their relationship. What is noteworthy, is that
Jude, who didn't know Wadleigh well, seems more ready with
hospitality as well as medical care and kindness for Mr. Wadleigh
than does John Blaisdell, Wadleigh's co-worker.

The above testimony shows Jude's neighbor referring to him
as "Captain," which may be due to his military service, which
was extensive. It wasn't until April 1818 that he began to receive
his government pension, granted in recognition of his years of
service in the early wars of our nation. Daniel Gookin, Esq.
was the recipient of his pension monies. According to Roland
Sawyer, historian for Kensington, Jude was thrown headlong by
a cannonball striking him during one of the battles of the Revolutionary War. That old injury finally caught up with him and
he died in 1828. He is buried in the northeast corner of the
Old Slave Yard in that town.[32] After his death, Rhoda moved to
Belfast, Maine, where she made application for the remainder of
his pension, which was granted her in 1830.

Life was hard for both the parents and the children in the
Hall family. Three of Rhoda and Jude's sons were kidnapped
and/or sold into slavery. James, at eighteen years of age was
kidnapped by David Wedgewood, who took him to Newburyport, Massachusetts. He was placed on board a ship bound for
New Orleans and there was sold to a Frenchman from Kentucky.
Aaron Hall was a seafarer and was kidnapped from Providence,
Rhode Island. By various turns, it ended up that he was sent
to sea and not heard from again by his family. Finally, William
sailed on the ship *Hannibal* from Newburyport, Massachusetts,

and was sold into slavery when the ship reached the West Indies. He escaped ten years later and earned a position as captain on a coal vessel operating along the coastline of England from Newcastle and London.[33]

Jude's grandsons Moses, Jude, and Aaron remained in the Exeter area. Years later they followed their grandfather's example and joined the service of their country in the Civil War.

On a side note, Jude Hall's first owner's father, Philemon Blake Sr. was born in Hampton in 1671. Philemon married Sarah Dearborn. In the Hampton Falls Church record of baptisms, it states that Jane, Negro to Philemon Blake Sr., was baptized in 1734. Philemon and Sarah had several children, among them Philemon Jr. who married Lydia Boulter in 1727 and settled in Kensington. It is not known if Jane moved into Philemon Jr.'s family following his father's death. It is also unknown whether Jane could have been related to Jude Hall—especially if he was born closer to 1755 than 1744.

Bess and Jack (Weare)

Nathaniel Weare born 1669, son of the Honorable Nathaniel Weare, became a deacon in the Hampton Congregational Church, having owned the covenant in 1697. Among other accomplishments, he was a justice of the Superior Court; was chosen speaker of the House of Representatives in 1727, and he built a mill in North Yarmouth, Maine. Nathaniel also owned a Negro, Jack, and an Indian woman, Bess.

One of Nathaniel's sons, John (b. 1696), married Deborah Taylor in 1720. They had, among other children, Jonathan, born 1724, who also became a deacon in the Hampton church. Jonathan married Sarah Lane in 1747 and they had five children.

A story is told of Jonathan's great-grandson, Colonel John Mitchell Weare (born 1814), who settled in Seabrook as a farmer. He was a justice of the peace and quorum throughout New

Hampshire and did quite a bit of probate work. Perhaps because of this work, he received an original bond, dated December 15, 1755, from Jeremiah Eastman of Kensington to Jonathan Weare, of Hampton Falls (great-grandfather of Colonel John Weare). The bond was worth a thousand pounds lawful money and was meant to be used for the care and support of "a Negro man Slave named Jack and an Indian woman slave named Bess, who were lately the servants of Nathaniel Weare late of Hampton Falls, deceased, for which said Jonathan Weare hath paid to said Jeremiah Eastman 500 old tenor."[34] The bond included enough funds to also cover a proper burial at their deaths. The bond was witnessed by Meshech Weare and his wife, Mehetabel (Wainwright) Weare.

Of all of the named slaves who appeared in Hampton Congregational records or in the records of the daughter and granddaughter churches, Bess, Syppio, Judith and her unnamed mother were the only named American Indian slaves who appeared in the Hampton Falls records, along with Margaret Prince and her mother mentioned earlier in the Hampton Records.

Meshech Weare, who witnessed this bond, was uncle to Jonathan and is also listed in the Hampton Falls church records as owning a slave, a Negro man, James, who was baptized and owned the covenant in 1739.[35] Meshech was deeply appreciated by his fellow townsfolk who elected him again and again as a representative to the General Court. In 1754, he became a colonel in the militia and was appointed a delegate from New Hampshire to the Albany convention to secure some safety against the French and to investigate whether an alliance could be had with the Indians. Colonel Meshech Weare was eventually elected, as soon as the state constitution was adopted, the first president of New Hampshire. It is not known whether Meshech still owned James on becoming New Hampshire's first president.

Timothy Nokes

Timothy Nokes was perhaps the son of Cuffee Noaks (spellings here are given as in the records), a tanner, who sold ten acres of land to William Pottle in 1753. William Pottle was a blacksmith, the son of the Christopher Pottle who bought of Mr. Tobias Langdon of Portsmouth, an unnamed black youth in 1699. Cuffee Nokes is believed to have been a free black and was a soldier in the French and Indian War. Salisbury Vital Records reveal a marriage between Coffe Noakes and Lidia Moody in 1743, and Timothy must have been their son. He was living in Kensington when he enlisted in the military as his father had. Perhaps because he would have lived as a free black, Timothy, like many free blacks living without land, lived in poverty. In 1774, he had been warned out of Kensington along with Ebenezer Mingo.[36] Timothy must have imagined that enlisting in military service was one way of earning money, so, in 1775, he did just that and was sent to Winter Hill, near Boston. The list of those who served with Capt. Stephen Clark's company at Winter Hill includes not only Timothy but also Caesar Macling, listed above under Hampton. Timothy enlisted a second time and served for Massachusetts rather than New Hampshire. He saw little duty because four months into this second enlistment, he died in June of 1777. Little is known of Timothy's family, or indeed, if he even was married.[37]

The African Americans of the Daughter Church of North Hampton

Members of First Congregational Church of Hampton began petitioning the church for a dismissal in order to form a parish at North Hill in 1719. In May of that year, the frame of a new meeting house for the use of First Church in Hampton was raised. Three months later, the first family, the Thomas Marstons, were dismissed to North Hill by the council. Six months later, Thomas Robie and John Cogswell followed and the slow drip of dismissals continued as the North Hill Parish began to take shape. The North Hill meeting house was readied by 1734 and the first meeting held in 1738. It would be another four years, however, before the town of North Hampton was granted its charter by Governor Benning in 1742.

Although the settlers who left Hampton did so in the early years of the eighteenth century, the records of the church of North Hampton began listing baptisms of African Americans toward the middle of that century.

Dinah (Wingate)

Dinah, Negro of Colonel Wingate's was baptized in October of 1752.[38] Dinah later married Prince Whipple. Her story covers several generations and appears in the Hampton church section of this work.

Dinah, George, and Phillis (Dearborn)

A servant, also named Dinah, was baptized in 1754[39] and worked for Mr. Joseph Dearborn. This Dinah had a story much less lengthy than Dinah Whipple's. Joseph was the son of Deacon John Dearborn and was born about 1696. He married Anna Dearborn in 1719 and lived at North Hampton until his death in 1768. All that is clear concerning Joseph's servant, Dinah is that she was baptized fourteen years before Joseph died—whether as a child or an adult is not clear—and that she lived for a time in North Hampton. There is no certainty that she was of African origin and no certainty whether she was slave or free. In his will, it states that Joseph Dearborn gives his wife Anna, "My maid servant"[40] without any indication whether this servant was Dinah or again, whether she was African American or not. However, because she was given as part of Joseph's legacy, it is likely she was not free.

Among Joseph and Anna's seven children was Levi, born in 1730. Levi graduated from Harvard and became a well-respected physician in North Hampton. On August 17 and 31 of 1755 respectively, George, Negro man of Dr. (Levi) Dearborn and Phillis, daughter of Dr. Dearborn's Negro man were baptized.[41] The record does not indicate Phillis's age when she was baptized. But it is possible that Dinah and George were parents of Phillis. If this is true, it is an unusual example of an entire African American family living together in the same household. William Cotton, of Portsmouth, was one of the few leading men of his community to own a whole family of slaves, and this might be a similar situation.

Anna Dearborn died in 1789 and by 1795, Dr. Levi Dearborn had sold Dinah, George, and Phillis to Amos Seavey (joiner), father-in-law of Elizabeth Garland Seavey. There is a single line in the Town Records of North Hampton that says, "Dinah (a black) dies, December 1799." There is no way to verify who is meant by this particular Dinah, but it could have been Joseph Dearborn's servant, Dinah, who was owned by Amos Seavey by 1799.

Nathaniel, Servant of Stephen Batchelder

"Nathaniel, servant of Stephen Batchelder" [was baptized in March of 1756].[42] This record does not state Nathaniel's age, race, or whether he was slave or free. Little else is known about Nathaniel, except the fact of a possible marriage recorded in the town records between a "Neatheniel and a Saley Tuck," both of Hampton, in 1787. Even here there is no adjective describing either one of them.

Peter, Servant of John Wingate

Other records are similarly silent on the same details. For example, in 1779, Peter, servant of John Wingate, is baptized. He is identified as "black" only in another source.[43] Peter, listed here in North Hampton's church records may be the same Peter whom Paine Wingate speaks of remembering growing up in his grandfather's home.

Kitterick/Kittery and Peggy Tuckerman

In 1778, Kitterick Tuckerman of Portsmouth is recorded as being united in marriage to Peggy Leavitt of North Hampton by Rev. McClure. Three years later in 1781, Kittery, an infant son of Kitterick and Peg Tuckerman, died. (Rye records Kittery's death as 1780.) Then in 1782, Peg Tuckerman (a Negro woman) is baptized just prior to her death. Kitterick's death is recorded in Portsmouth records as happening in 1788. The spelling is, Kittery, but it most likely refers to Kitterick the father.[44]

It is unclear whether Kitterick (or Kittery), the father, is actually "Kittindge" Tuckerman, one of the signers to a petition made to the New Hampshire General Assembly in 1779 by several slaves for their freedom. The petition states in part:

> [We] Natives of Africa, now forcably detained in Slavery in said State most humbly Sheweth, That the God of Nature, gave them, Life, and Freedom, upon the Terms of the most perfect Terms of the most perfect Equality with other men; That Freedom is an inherent Right of the human Species, not to

be surrendered, but by the Consent, for the Sake of social Life; That private or publick Tyranny, and Slavery, are alike detestable to Minds, conscious of the equal Dignity of human Nature; That, in Power and Authority of Individuals, derived solely from a Principle of Coercion, against the Will of Individuals, and to dispose of their Persons and Properties, consists the compleatest Idea of private and political Slavery.[45]

If Kittery is Kittindge Tuckerman, petition signer, it feels right that after all these years, after the loss of both his wife and son within the first four years of his marriage, that his poignant plea for freedom was granted in June 2013, when Governor Maggie Hassan, put her signature on a bill to grant this petition. What a gift to his son, to have signed his name to this petition before his son was ever born. (Prince Whipple was another signer of this petition, husband to Dinah Chase, listed under the Hampton section.)

Peter Kent

Peter Kent is another African whose name appears in the North Hampton history but not in the North Hampton church records. In 1775 Peter served for North Hampton in the third New Hampshire Regiment at the Battle of Bunker Hill. He is listed as being paid for his first month's service and receiving his coat money. These are the slimmest of gleanings about his life until 1810 when he appears on the North Hampton pauper rolls. The selectmen paid him twenty-nine cents per week until the end of the year when he moved to Deerfield, New Hampshire.[46]

Peter Grant

Peter Grant is yet a third *Peter* from North Hampton, and he is also not listed in the church record. The *New Hampshire Gazette* ran this ad in 1769 regarding Peter Grant, who was owned by Jonathan Knowles Jr. It does not specify that Peter is an African American, simply a "servant." However, it is probable that he was an African American and that he was returned, because there is a record of Peter enlisting in the army under Capt. Nathaniel Rand. "Forgotten Black Patriots" is an extensive compilation of Black Soldiers done by the DAR and Peter Grant appears in this work as an African man. Perhaps this was Peter's first attempt to enlist?

> RANAWAY from Jonathan Knowls, junr. in North-Hampton, the 12th of this Instant, a servant BOY named Peter Grant, about 16 Years of Age, a short thick set Fellow: Had on when he went away, a cloth-color'd homespun Coat and Jacket; Leather Breeches and Yarn Stockings; Whoever takes up said Runaway and coneys him safe to his Master, shall have Two Shillings Reward paid by JONATHAN KNOWLS, jun. N.B. All Masters of Vessels and others are forbid harbouring, concealing, or carrying off said Servant, as they would avoid Trouble.[47]

African Americans from the Records of Rye

There seem to have been three or four families in Rye who owned a number of slaves over the course of several years. These families were often related by marriage. Some of these slave holders and their slaves were connected to those in Hampton, despite the fact that Rye is not a daughter or granddaughter church of Hampton Congregational Church. The slaves who are listed below appear for two reasons. First, it took North Hampton almost twenty years to receive a release of its members from the Hampton church to found its church. During this time, Rye annexed hundreds of acres of land originally thought of as part of North Hampton. Secondly, there has been an exceptional amount of work done by Valerie Cunningham on the African American population of Portsmouth. Since Rye was originally also included in the land portion of North Hampton, it has an almost equally strong tie to this neighbor town to the south as it does to Portsmouth. However, not nearly as much work has been done on the African American population in Rye. Therefore, it is included here, in the hopes that someone will choose to do a more in-depth look in the future at this diverse and important segment of Rye's population.

The Seavey House located in Rye, near what is today Brackett Road. Photo courtesy of the Rye Historical Society

Slaves in the Seavey Family

Ammi or Amie

The first resident of the Seavey clan that prospered in Rye was William Seavey, born in 1648. When he died in 1733, it is said that he bequeathed a Negro slave woman, Ammi, to his loving wife Hannah.[48] In 1741, when Hannah (Jackson) Seavey died at age ninety, she bequeathed a cow to "Amie," her Negro woman.

Hampshire

William Seavey's grandson, Amos, born in 1718, owned several slaves, some of whom he bought of Dr. Dearborn. Amos also had at least six brothers, one of whom was William. In 1744, William gave a twelve-year-old Negro boy named "Hampshire," and some land to Amos Seavey. In 1756, Amos published a run-away slave notice in the *Boston Post*: "a likely lusty fellow, aged 23 born in New England, he has large long Feet and is about 5'10", has a good set of white teeth and a light complexion." Apparently, this runaway left carrying a heavy load as the ad goes on to detail three coats, two pairs of breeches (one leather), and three pairs of stockings. The reward was five dollars for returning said lusty fellow to Amos Seavey.[49] This run-away was likely Hampshire.

Peggy, Jenny, and Patience

In 1754, Peggy, a Negro child belonging to Amos Seavey, was baptized. Two more Negro children belonging to Amos Seavey were also baptized: Jenny, in 1760, and Patience, in 1768.[50] Several years later, Seavey noted in his journal, "Jennie, our negro woman, went away from us on the sabbath day morning, 1795."[51] One wonders whether Jennie, baptized in 1760, just prior to the Revolutionary War, had been given the option of her freedom as of that Sabbath morning in 1795, and decided to say, "yes," to a gift that simply allowed her to go away from the only family she may have known in Rye.

George, Phillis, and Dinah

George, Phillis, and Dinah, the previously mentioned Negro servants of Joseph and Levi Dearborn of North Hampton are also recorded in the Rye records as having been baptized, and George and Phillis owned the covenant.[52] Phillis and Dinah are listed in the North Hampton Congregational Church records in years (1754/5) as being baptized when they belonged to the Dearborns. They are listed in the Rye records with 1753 as the date for George and Phillis's baptisms and 1757 for Dinah's. It is likely that they are the same persons and that the difference in dates lies in record-keeping. In the Rye records they are owned by Amos Seavey. As difficult as it is to imagine being owned by another person, it may have been some consolation to have been able to stay together as a family; bought and also sold as a family while staying in the same geographical area.

Nero, John Sunday (or Sandy), Titus, and Dinah

In 1770, Nero, servant of James Seavey, was baptized. In 1772, "John Sunday [Sandy], a Negro man," was baptized along with Negro children, Titus and Dinah, who were brought to baptism by James Seavey.[53] Nero, John, Titus, and Dinah were all owned by James Seavey, son of James (born in 1721). We can be certain it was the son named James because James, his father, had died in 1755. John Sunday's baptism is also listed in North Hampton town records.

"Bow" and a Negro Boy

A Negro called "Bow" and another Negro boy are also named in the Rye town history as belonging to the same James Seavey, who brought them to church in 1806 for baptism. This was a full thirty years after the Revolutionary War had ended. Of the slaves listed in the nine towns included in this work, these two men are among the very few African Americans who were still enslaved into the first decade of the nineteenth century.

Cato (Seavey)

Cato Seavey (colored man) dies on April 4, 1829 at age of 98-108 years.[54]

I could find no other information about Cato in the Rye town or church records. However, several of the African Americans listed in this work died between 1820 and 1830, well-advanced in years. It is possible, given Cato Seavey's age as listed, that William Seavey, who was the first Seavey in Rye, could have owned Cato. William bequeathed his servant Ammi to his wife upon his death and it could be that Ammi was Cato's mother. One might imagine this was why Hannah Seavey, William's wife, left Ammi a cow when she died, so Cato would survive as long as he did!

Jack (Odiorne)

Jack was a Negro man owned by Madame Philip Odiorne, or Elizabeth Odiorne, who was William Seavey's sister. Jack was said to have married "one of James Seavey's negresses." However, there is no record of Jack's marriage to Dinah who belonged to James. James did own several children, such as Titus and Dinah, who might have been born of such a marriage, however. Jack was involved with the yearly Black Coronations, which took place in Portsmouth, elected often to the position of sheriff.[55] As elected leader, a slave like Jack served as judge or mediator on behalf of the African American community.

Garland Family Slaves

Black Prince

In the Garland genealogy, we read that when Colonel Benjamin Garland returned from the Revolutionary war, he brought with him a black servant called, "Black Prince" whom he had bought for a keg of rum.[56] Prince apparently asked at one point if he could go for a few days to visit family in Rhode Island. Benjamin granted him permission and he returned in due time. Time passed, and Black Prince asked if he could go again to visit family. Again, Benjamin agreed only this time Black Prince did not "come home" and Benjamin offered a reward for his return. A 1783 newspaper ad in Rhode Island reads:

> [A] lusty stout Negro Man...about 5 feet 9 or 10 inches high, goes a little limping, one of his ankles being considerably larger than the other, plays well on a fiddle . . . Had on, when he went away, a felt hat, a whitened tow-cloth shirt and linen stock, a brown homespun close bodied coat, an old light coloured great-coat, a new white, short, woolen homespun jacket, with a belt to it; a pair of full cloth homespun gray breeches, black and white yarn stockings.

The notice gives warning to vessels and also notes, "He had enlisted on board a Privateer at Newport, but inquiry being made for him, he left here and 'tis supposed he is gone to Providence or Boston to look for a voyage to sea, for which he has a great inclination" Ten dollars if found in Rhode Island, Twenty dollars if found elsewhere. Benjamin Garland."[57]

When John Garland came to the Hampton area in 1653, he settled in the eastern part of the town. Nearly forty years later, John Garland's great-grandson, Benjamin, who was, as stated earlier, a colonel in the Revolutionary War, settled in Rye as had his father. He was born in 1734, and married Sarah Jenness. He was an innkeeper, and he and Sarah had several children.

Abigail, Benjamin's daughter, married Jonathan Jenness and a second daughter of Benjamin's, Elizabeth, married Joseph Seavey, son of Amos Seavey. Just ahead, other stories of inter-family marriages of slave-owning families are mentioned: Jenness with Seavey, Parsons with Seavey, and Garland with Seavey, to name a few. Inter-family marriages make it difficult in certain cases to tease apart the web of connections that existed not only among these families but also among the African slaves they owned. This was especially true since often at the time of marriage a slave was transferred from one family to another as a "wedding gift." This was likely the case when Martha Seavey, daughter of Amos, married Benjamin Jenness and received a "black slave and a black cow." Also, the Jenness family owned a slave named Prince, and it may be that Benjamin Garland's slave "Black Prince" might be the same person as Job Jenness's servant, Prince. This suggestion could be laid alongside Glenn Knoblock's suggestion that Prince Jenness and Prince Liberty were one in the same person.[58]

George

In 1783, "George a Negro boy," was baptized under the name Garland. There is no further information about his age or even which member of the Garland family sponsored him for baptism. Benjamin Garland's daughter, Sarah, managed both the house and farm on her own and may have needed the help of this boy, George.

Slaves in the Jenness Family of Rye

Paul and Prince, Blacks; Old Black Peter; Caesar Jenness[59]

Jeb Jenness gave his slaves, Paul and Prince, their freedom to enlist in the Revolutionary War. Likely the Prince named here was also known as Prince Jenness and is one of the Rye men listed as "being lost in the War," as was his master, Job Jenness, who died at Valley Forge in 1777. Knoblock posits that Prince Jenness may have adopted the last name of Liberty since a Prince Liberty's death is recorded in 1777, as was Prince Jenness's death. Paul Jenness may be one and the same person as Paul (Pasol) Long whose story is told above in connection with Caesar, George, and Alice Long. There is a marriage record of a Caesar Jenness and Molly Downe in 1797 in Portsmouth, but by 1820, Caesar Jenness was living alone in North Hampton next door to William Scott, also black. This Caesar may have been related to Paul Jenness (Long) since there is a Caesar Long who was Paul's brother. Or, if Prince Jenness and Prince Liberty are one in the same, might Caesar Jenness, who is listed in North Hampton records, have also chosen to become Caesar Liberty? If that were so, it might explain a connection to the record of Caesar Liberty who marries Phebe Ozel in 1783, which appears later in the work.[60]

"Old Black Peter" lived in a house near the blacksmith shop at Rye Center, built for Eben Berry. It is unknown to whom this record refers. The record shows that Peter was of African origin and that he was free if living by himself, but nothing more is certain. He may have belonged to Mr. Wingate in North Hampton, who owned a slave named Peter. But the house near the blacksmith shop was also occupied by Reuel Garland and Albert Walker, among others, so Old Black Peter may have had some connections with the Garland family who owned Black Prince.

Samuel Wallis's Slaves

Caesar and Phillis[61]

Samuel Wallis was born about 1717. He was the son of Samuel and Hannah (Seavey) Wallis. About 1743 he married Sarah Moses. Samuel was listed as residing in Rye in the 1790 census and his household included: three men over 16, two females, and one other person. This "other" was likely an African American. In Samuel's will dated 16 October 1793, he gives his Negro "Philless" to his son, Samuel, born 1747.[62] Phillis was about eight or nine years of age when she was purchased and brought to Rye in 1750 by mariner Alexander Raitt of New Castle. She grew up on the Wallis farm, eventually working alongside Caesar, who was born about 1740. Phillis may actually have been purchased by Rev. Samuel Parsons. She came to his home by way of Mr. Raitt, through Joseph Newmarch, minister in Kittery, Maine. Elizabeth, daughter of Rev. Parsons, married Samuel Wallis in 1773, so she would have been at the Wallis Sands farm when Caesar arrived in 1778. Elizabeth's dower may have included Phillis being sent from Rev. Parsons, Elizabeth's father, to Samuel Wallis, her husband (although this is not recorded anywhere). If Phillis is, then, the "other, non-white" listed in the 1790 census and not listed as "slave" it may be that Phillis had been given her freedom by then. Many had already been freed in the post-Revolutionary years, but had also decided to remain with their slave-holding families.

Caesar Wallis used the alias of Caesar Seavey. Wallis purchased Caesar from an agent, Captain William Parker, who was a schooner master, in 1778. Almost immediately, Caesar tried to run away, as reported in this ad from the Freeman's Journal, May 12, 1778:

> Ran away Saturday the 9th inst. A Negro Man
> named Caesar, from his Master Sam Wallis of Rye -
> 35 Years of Age- Five Feet and a half high; had on
> when he went away a blue Kersey Coat, grey home-
> spun Breeches and grey Stockings - Whoever takes up
> said Negro and returns him to his Master shall have
> Twenty Dollars Reward."[63]

Twenty dollars was not an insignificant amount in that era! But someone must have walked away fingering that money. Caesar made his way back to Samuel Wallis, where he continued to live, perhaps going back and forth between the Wallis and Seavey families, since Hannah, Samuel's mother, was a Seavey. This would account for only one "other" being mentioned in the 1790 census, if Caesar was at Seavey's homestead on census day.

Caesar married a woman named Phillis, who was also owned by Samuel Wallis. This could well be the Phillis who was likely given to Samuel Wallis by Samuel Parsons. Caesar and Phillis were both granted their freedom and tried relocating to Salem, Massachusetts, but in the end they returned to Rye and the Wallis farm. Although we do not know their age at marriage, Caesar died at eighty-one years of age and Phillis at age eighty, in or near 1821. Both were buried on the Wallis homestead.[64]

There is historical evidence that a second Caesar Wallis (Wallace) existed. This Caesar Wallis married Katy Duce in 1783 and it is possible that his son, Caesar, was the Wallace warned out of Exeter in 1842, with family: George, James, Freeman, Catherine, and Dolly Pauls Wallis.[65] Charles Bell's list of Exeter marriages includes the union of George Wallace and Dolly Pauls in 1818 as well as Catharine Wallace and Jacob Pauls, Jr. in 1813. This second Caesar hailed from Meredith and served in the Revolutionary War. He was discharged in New Windsor, New York in 1783 and his discharge papers were said to have been signed by George Washington.[66]

Libby Family Slaves

Gloucester, Negro child of Joseph Libbey[67]

Another family in Rye who had some connection to the Hampton Church families was that of Joseph Libbey. He was the grandson of Anthony Libby of Hampton. Joseph was born in a part of Hampton that eventually was incorporated into Rye. In 1749, Joseph Libbey had a Negro child, "Gloucester," baptized in the Rye Congregational Church. This baptism would have taken place about the same time that Joseph's son, Abraham, would have been baptized had he lived more than a few days after his birth.

In a list of African-American soldiers who fought in the Revolution, a Gloster Watson's name appears. Glenn Knoblock states that Gloster was owned by Joseph Libby at the time of his baptism, which Knoblock records as taking place in Portsmouth. Libbey sold Gloster to Dudley Watson of Dover. Gloster was freed by Dudley Watson's son in 1777, but his manumission was also helped along by the preaching of Rev. Jeremy Belknap, who was a strong abolitionist. Gloster served for three years as a soldier, saw a great deal of action, and when he died, in 1806 at the age of fifty-seven, there was an obituary in the local paper—a rare honor that was not usually granted to a former slave.[68]

Additional African Americans Appearing in the Rye Town Records

Of the remaining names of African Americans who are connected with families not listed in the Rye Congregational Church records, only one has roots back into the families who made up the First Congregational Church of Hampton. His name is found in a New England Chronicle notice, first posted in 1775, concerning the run-away slave Peter Long, bought of Samuel Whidden by Merryfield Berry. If Peter Long and Paul Long are one in the same person, then Peter is connected to Caesar Long of Hampton, mentioned earlier.

The following list of names that includes identifying adjectives such as "black" or "Negro," appear in the Rye vital records with some of the same names appearing in the North Hampton vital records. The records are brief and offer little in the way of hints as to who certain individuals were. The records are included because often church records only include dates of baptisms, marriages, or admittances to full Communion. Town records include dates of births, deaths and gestures of charity toward the poor. Rye Town records are included, as well, because Rye struggled for decades to define its borders with the older towns of North Hampton and Hampton. Rye also struggled for decades to be seen as other than a "parish" aligned with New Castle. This struggle affected their delegate representation to political conventions and meant that their identity as an independent community was always at risk as boundaries were continually in dispute from every side. Several times Rye residents petitioned the legislature for rights as a town instead of a parish, and for relief from the oversight of New Castle. Not until 1785, by action of the legislature, did Rye become a town and then Rye never looked back to its old identity as parish. Therefore, the Rye town records listed here cover that long time of struggle from 1774, through the declaration of "township" and on into the early nineteenth century. The struggle of Rye mirrors, in a small way, the struggle of African Americans to define who they were vis-à-vis all others around them.

- In 1774, Dinah, wife of Caesar, dies. It is unclear who Caesar is in this case. It is possible that he is Caesar Long.

This record also appears in North Hampton records.

- In 1783, Caesar Liberty and Phebe Ozel (probably colored) married. Phebe Ozel is listed as teaching needlework after 1779 in a local school in Rye. Phebe had a son, Benoni, a mulatto who was born in Rye in 1757. Phebe was said to have lived until the age of eighty-two years, dying in Rye in 1820. Phebe and Caesar may have had a second son, Caesar Liberty, who found his way to Scroon, New York, for there is a Caesar who is in the 1860 New York compiled census records as living by himself.[69]

- In 1799, "Dinah (black) dies." In the North Hampton church records, Dinah (black) is recorded as dying in 1794 and it is clearer in that account that she is likely the wife of Caesar Long, who died of alcoholism. This account gives no such information.

- William Varrell fought in the Revolutionary War for six months beginning in 1776 in Pierce Long's Regiment. William was only fifteen or sixteen years old at the time. He saw service in New Castle and West Point, and married Lydia Currier, from Portsmouth in 1800.[70] He may have been the son of Elizabeth Varrell, listed as being baptized in Hampton Falls.

African Americans from the Daughter Church at Kingston

On September 25, 1725, it is recorded in Volume I & II of the Hampton Church records these minutes of a church meeting:

> Were dismissed from this Church in order to their being incorporated into a Church State at Kingstown. Ichabod Robie, Jonathan and Elizabeth

Sanborn, Aaron Sleeper, Moses and Alma Elkins, Thomas Webster, Sarah Fifeld and Moses Sleeper.[71]

Much earlier, in 1694, a small group of Hampton residents had petitioned the governor and council to become a township, using land in the western part of the town. Their request was granted. On August 6, 1694, the new town was incorporated, and named Kingstown. Eventually, East Kingston, Danville (formerly Hawke), and Sandown would be formed from this first grant. Rev. Ward Clark was called as the first ordained pastor of the Kingston Parish, following Mr. Choate, who served nearly a decade as a lay supply preacher, and Mr. Thompson, who served briefly. During the ministries of Benjamin Choate and Mr. Thompson between 1707 and 1725, there are few if any records that remain today of those who were baptized or joined the church. This may not be entirely due to a lax attitude toward record-keeping on their parts, for the town of Kingston lived for many years in turmoil. Considered a frontier town, Kingston residents were embroiled in defending their settlement against the French and Indians for nearly two decades before they were able to sign a peace treaty and determine how they could afford to call a settled, ordained pastor. Rev. Ward Clark was their choice and he was ordained in 1725. At his service were many of the same men who had been present at the founding of the parish at Hampton Falls. Also present at the service might have been his two slaves, sitting in the balcony observing the service and the new faith community, perhaps wondering about whether they would ever partake in its welcoming sacraments.

Rev. Clark was a vigorous man, well loved, and one who was quite instrumental in the growing of both congregation and town. He is remembered for growing the size of the faith community by relaxing the rigid requirements of church membership as well as planting the first elms that provided shade for the barren plains that served as the town's landscape. His career was cut short when the throat distemper hit Kingston. He succumbed to the disease, exhausted from tending his wife and two children who died just before him. In his will, Rev. Clark left his two Negro servants to his brother and sister for seven years, and at the end of that time, to be well-clothed and set free of their bondage.[72]

The Kingston Ecclesiastical Society called Rev. Joseph Seacomb in 1737 upon the death of Rev. Clark. He was known as a good man, a poor man's son. The church grew rapidly under his shepherding and in 1739, the East Kingston church split off with Danville and Hawke coming later, in 1756 and 1760. Rev. Amos Tappan followed Rev. Seacomb in 1760 and served for nine years. One of the last pastors of notable repute was Rev. Elihu Thayer whose ministry began in 1776 and included the founding of the New Hampshire Missionary Society in 1801, of which he was its first president.

In the records of baptisms left by Rev. Joseph Seacomb there appear several baptisms of African Americans. Rev. Seacomb was born in Boston and ordained in 1733. He began life as a fisherman before he felt called to "become a fisher of men." He first chose to spread the knowledge of Christ and to carry the gospel to the aboriginal nations who surrounded the borders of New England. However, in 1737, he felt called to Kingston and there he started his ministry. Ironically, he records no Native Americans among the baptized. There are, however, several names of African Americans. Few of these names leave clues that might help in giving a fuller picture of any of these individuals. Therefore, they are simply listed with brief sketches of their owners. The earliest mention of an African American in the Kingston Church is a death in records kept by Rev. Ward Clark.

Unnamed Negro Boy (Eastman/Easeman)

[In 1731] "Decemr ye 11 Ebenezer Easeman lost a negro boy."[73]
Ebenezer Eastman or Easeman was born in 1701. He married
Mary Sleeper in 1726 in Kingston, he coming from Salisbury
and she from Hampton. Among their children, there were three
sons, Edward, Samuel, and Ebenezer, born in 1729. It is likely
that Ebenezer, the father, is the one referenced in this record of
the Negro boy's death. It is unclear how this Negro boy died. It
was in May of 1735 that the throat distemper epidemic began
and in the first month it caused the deaths of twenty-six people.
It peaked in early 1736, but by then nearly one thousand people
had died. This phrase also does not specifically say that this
Negro boy was a slave of Mr. Easeman.

Unnamed Slave (Choate)

[In 1734] "May ye 13 Mr. Choate lost an Negroe an Old man."[74]

Mr. Benjamin Choate, a Harvard educated man, was an
evangelical preacher in Kingston for many years, although never
ordained. Born in 1680 to John and Ann Choate, he moved to
Kingston in 1707, when he was called as pastor. He continued to
reside in town for many years after he left the church. Although
the name of the old Negro man who died in 1734 is not listed
here, nor the reason for his death, what is here is a piece of
a long record of slave-owning in the Choate family, beginning with Governor Thomas Choate of Hogg Island, Ipswich,
Massachusetts.

The first mention of slaves in the Choate family is a bill
of sale, dated July 30, 1717, that states that Governor Thomas
Choate, Benjamin's brother, sold to Jonathan Bunker of Charles-
town, "a negro" whom he had bought from Joshua Norwood of
Gloucester. When Thomas Choate was a member of the General
Court he bought off Long Wharf in Boston "a negro boy just

arrived from Africa by the name of Ned" for his son, Francis. At the time of this purchase, Benjamin had already been preaching in Kingston about ten years and may only have met Ned when Benjamin visited his brother at Hogg Island. But Ned later married Sabina (Binah), a Negro slave whom Thomas acquired from Robert Choate of Ipswich in exchange for one, "Phillis," another Negro slave. Ned became a member of a church and eventually he and Sabina grew a family of seven children: Edward, Titus, Peter, Caezar, Jane, Violet, and Peggy. Ned and Binah were given their freedom when Thomas died in 1745, but they stayed with the Choate family, which was common given that a freed slave did not own land and sometimes not even a home for his or her family. Ned stayed with Francis Choate even after Governor Choate moved off Hogg Island. Ned died on the island in 1800 at age ninety. Several of his children went as slaves to other members of the Choate family including Isaac, and John, Esquire. Two of Ned's sons stayed with Thomas and are buried on Hogg Island. Jane and Violet, Ned's daughters, died young.[75] None of Ned and Binah's children went to Benjamin in Kingston, which might have provided a name for the old Negro man who died in 1734.

Segoa (Blaisdell)

[In 1742] "Segoa, Negro boy servant to Jona Blaisdell" was baptized]. Jonathan Blaisdell was born in 1709 in Amesbury, Massachusetts, and married Hannah Jones in 1731. Segoa was likely the first Negro child baptized by Rev. Seacomb.

Benoni (Hubbard)

[In 1743] "Benoni, Infant Servant of Deacon Hubbard" [was baptized]. One may assume that Benoni was of African descent from this short entry in Rev. Seacomb's record. The term, "infant servant" was a euphemism used to identify an African

American slave who was purchased as an infant. Deacon Jeremiah Hubbard would have been obligated to provide food, shelter, and clothing to his "infant servant" Benoni in return for small tasks around the house—more and more of which could be accomplished as Benoni grew. Whether or what Jeremiah eventually paid Benoni for his services is not known, but payment should not have changed the set of obligations attendant upon Mr. Hubbard to care for his servant, nor his liability for harming the infant servant.

Coffee, or Cuffee (Stevens)

[In 1744 (Coffee) or] "Cuffee, Negro Servant of Ebenezer Stevens" [was baptized]. Cuffee (Stevens) does not appear anywhere else in connection with Ebenezer Stevens, although there is a chance that Caesar and Cato (Stevens) both slaves belonging to Ebenezer's family may have known Cuffee. Cuffee may also have known Dinah, who joined the Stevens slaves, along with Caesar, sometime after 1768.

Mary (Hunton)

[In 1754] "Mary, Infant Servant of John Hunton" [was baptized]. John Hunton, son of Philip Hunton and Betsy Hall, was born in 1690 in Exeter and married Mary Rundlett. They lived in Kingston and had twelve children. John died in 1778 and Daniel, his son, and Mary, his wife, died in 1735 of throat distemper. John's brother, Samuel, was killed by Indians. It is unknown what became of Mary after so many died in the Hunton family. It is again, unclear whether Mary was of African descent from this record, although likely, since she, too, is an infant servant like Benoni.

Prince (Seacomb)

[In 1756] "Prince, my Negro, own'd the Covenant" [became a covenant member and was baptized] (written by Rev. Seacomb).

In 1760, four years after Prince had been baptized and joined the church, Rev. Seacomb died. There is no mention in the probate records of Prince being sold to anyone else and since Rev. Seacomb had only one child, it is possible that Prince was granted his freedom. Mrs. Seacomb would have had to vacate the home given to the pastor following her husband's death, so it is likely that neither she nor Prince would have continued to live in a setting provided for by the church at Kingston.

Caesar (French)

[In 1756] "Caesar, Infant servant of Ensign French" [was baptized]. Once again, it is likely that Caesar was of African descent. The name "Caesar" was given to slaves or servants of African descent and "infant servant" almost always was a reference to a very young slave. Ensign Nathaniel French was the son of Nathaniel French, both of whom lived in Kingston. Since Caesar is not baptized until 1756, six years after father Nathaniel dies, Caesar definitely grew up in Ensign Nathaniel's home and could have been with him for many years, since he died in 1791.

Celia (Tole)

[In 1759] "Celia, negro servant-maid of Mr. Tole"[was baptized].[76] Celia may have been the maid-servant for Caleb Towle, grandson of Philip Towle who arrived in Hampton in 1659. Caleb settled in Kingston (which became Hawke) and had five children, one of whom was also Caleb. When Celia was baptized in 1759, Caleb (grandson) would have been eighty-one years old. His probated will of 1763, however, has no mention of Celia, nor does the will of Caleb (great grandson) who died in 1765.

African Americans in Kingston Town Records

Seco (Currier/Barnard)

In some copies of the New Hampshire Census of 1790, it appears that there is an unamed slave listed as a member of the Ezra Currier household living in Kingston.[77] But we do know that earlier, in 1777, a Ruth Currier deeded her Negro slave, Seco, to Joseph Barnard. Ruth drew up this deed on the day she died and Phebe Currier, her daughter-in-law, witnessed it. The copy of the deed reads this way:

> Know all men by These Presents that I Ruth Currier Relict of John Currier late of Kingston in the state of New Hampshire in New England Deceased for and in consideration of the Sum of Twenty Seven pounds L M To me in hand before ye Delivery hereof Well and truly paid by Joseph Barnard of d of Hopkinton in the State of New Hampshire aforesaid The receipt whereof I do acknowledge Have Given granted Bargained and Sold and by these Presents Do give grant Bargain Sell Convey and Confirm unto the Said Joseph Barnard his heirs and assigns forever a Certain Negro man Named Seco aged about thirty years of age Said Negro was given to me in the last Will and Testament of my late husband John Currier Late of Kingston deceased. To Have and to Hold the Said Negro to him the said Joseph Barnard his heirs and assigns to his & their only proper use Benefit forever and I the Said Ruth Currier for myself my

heirs Executors and administrators do hereby Covenant Grant and agree to and with the said Joseph
Barnard his heirs & assigns that until the Delivery
hereof I am the lawful owner of the said Negro and
am lawfully Seized and possessed of him in my own
Right in Fee Simple and have full power and Lawful
authority to Grant & Convey him in manner aforesaid an yt I and my heirs Executors & Administrators shall and will warrant to said Negro to the said
Barnard his heirs & assign agt the lawful Claims &
demands of any Person or Persons Whomsoever I
Witness whereof I have hereunto set my hand & Seal
this twenty ninth Day of March Annoque Domini
1777. Her[e] Signed sealed and Delivered Ruth X
Currier. mark in presence of us (L.S.) Elijah Clough/
Phebe Currier[78]

Ruth Currier was the mother of Captain Ezra Currier. Ezra,
who was born in Kingston in 1745, served in the Revolutionary
War and married Mehitable Eaton. Ezra's brother, John, born
in 1752, was also a captain in the army and had married Phebe
Witcher, who is likely the "Phebe Currier," Ezra's sister-in-law,
who witnessed the deed transferring ownership of Seco to
Joseph Barnard of Hopkinton. It is possible that Joseph Barnard
did not immediately take possession of Seco, and that Seco is
the slave listed in the 1790 census of Ezra Currier's household.
However, this seems unlikely given that Joseph Barnard lived
on his father Nathaniel's homestead in Hopkinton, worked
tirelessly to improve the homestead, and would have benefitted
from slave labor. It is more likely that John and Ruth Currier
had more than one slave. John Currier died in 1758, when
Ezra was thirteen years old, so Ezra would not have immediately become a slave owner. It is more reasonable to assume that

another unnamed slave, perhaps Seco's wife, stayed with Ruth until 1777 and then remained with the Ezra Currier family upon Ezra's return from military service.

Sometime after 1790, Ezra and Joseph Barnard freed Seco and his wife. Like so many other freed slaves, Seco apparently slipped into poverty and was warned out of Poplin (Fremont) in 1796 along with Phillis Currier who was likely his wife, and Phillip, a son.[79] Later, Seco and Phillis appear on the pauper rolls in Kingston[80] and later still, in 1850, a Polly Currier (Negro) was warned out of East Kingston and asked to move along so she might not end up burdening the town with her upkeep.[81] The date of 1850 makes it likely that Phillip was a son of Seco and Phillis, and that Polly was their grand-daughter.

Scipio Brown

Scipio Brown was born around 1738 and was a servant of Nathaniel Brown of Salisbury, Massachusetts. After Nathaniel died, Scipio became a free man and, in a rare series of documents, we can detail several land transactions that Scipio was involved in during the four or five years prior to the Revolutionary War. Twice in June of 1762 he purchased shares in the township of Gilmanton, partnering with James Tappin of Kingston. In 1764 he bought land in Raymond from Edward Scribner. In a second transaction in 1764, partnering this time with Ephraim Currier, he bought from Scribner part of a saw mill in Raymond. Two years later, in 1766, he sold forty acres of land in Raymond.[82] At some point, however, Scipio's fortunes reversed, for on January 3, 1769, he was warned out of Kingston, having traveled there from East Kingston.[83]

Scipio enlisted in 1775 and was first stationed at New Castle. He re-enlisted in 1776 and again was at New Castle on Great Island. One source lists Scipio as deserting the Continental service near the end of 1777. The truth is that Scipio had become ill while at Albany, New York. It is not known whether he survived to head home again to Kingston.[84]

Peter Bartlett/Peter Freeman

Peter Bartlett was the slave of Josiah Bartlett, one of the signers of the Declaration of Independence. Josiah was born in Ames- bury, Massachusetts, but before the age of twenty-one he had moved to Kingston to set up his medical practice. Ironically, Josiah was still a slave owner when he signed the Declaration. Peter, his slave, had begun to go by the name, Peter Freeman. Bartlett was enjoined in military action early in the war. He wrote home often to his wife, and in one letter asked that Peter "take good care of the cattle," to "not waste hay," and to "behave well" until his return.[85] Apparently, Peter had other ideas about how to "behave well" as he is listed as a runaway in early 1776. He must have drifted back to the Kingston area, because later, in 1780, he enlisted in the Continental Army and served for three years. In the 1800 New Hampshire Census of Rock- ingham County, he is listed as living with Josiah Bartlett and perhaps had not yet lived into the truth of the name he wished for as his own, "Free man."

Primus Lane/Prince or Primus Coffin

Primus Lane, who also went by the names Prince and Primus Coffin, was a noted violin player. He was owned by two different persons: Zaccheus Clough of Lee, and Rev. Peter Coffin of Kingston. The Coffin family had roots in Exeter and Rev. Coffin's father, Eliphalet, was a slave owner, even unto his death in 1735. Eliphalet bequeathed to his wife, Judith, his "Molatto Girl named Jinn, Jinne and Negro Girl Named Peg." Next, he bequeathed, Jack, another slave, to son Peter by declaration in his will, but only after Mrs. Judith Coffin no longer needed him.[86]

    Rev. Peter Coffin became the pastor of the Kingston

church in 1740. It is unknown if Jack joined Rev. Peter and his family, but near this same time, Primus was acquired. Primus lived in the parsonage with the family, as Phillis Parson had done in the parsonage of Rev. Jeremiah Fogg, of Kensington. In an intimately detailed way, Rev. Coffin kept track of Primus' birthdays so as to celebrate them along with his children's birthdays.[87] This was definitely a rare occasion in the life of a slave, for many could only guess at their age, and few could remember the actual date of their birth. Near the end of Primus's life he was owned by another family member; Enoch Coffin of Epping. As of the 1790 New Hampshire census, Enoch Coffin is listed as owning one slave, most likely Primus. As noted in the North Hampton section, intermarrying between slave-holding families makes for a tangled web at times in terms of discovering how a slave made his or her way toward possible freedom. This is true in the Coffin family as well in that Eliphalet Coffin and his wife, Judith Coffin, were distant cousins, as was Enoch Coffin of Epping.

In terms of Primus' first owner, Zaccheus Clough, it is interesting to note that in 1790, a Zaccheus Clough hailing from the village of Hawke (modern-day Danville) is also listed as owning one slave. It is doubtful that his name was Primus or Prince. Zaccheus was married to Love Meader of Lee and was a blacksmith who served in 1766 as second lieutenant under Archelaus Wood during the French and Indian War. In 1775, the Provincial Congress suggested that several towns take a census of the exact number of inhabitants. The Exeter census reveals that there resided there 760 males plus 51 men who had "gone in the army," 892 females, and 38 "Negroes and slaves for life." The census was sworn to before the justice of the peace, one Zaccheus Clough.[88] Zaccheus was, perhaps, following in the public service steps of his father, Ichabod, whose name was one of the first on the voters list in 1727 for the town of Kingston.

But Zaccheus was counting "slaves for life" who never imagined their names on a list of citizens who could vote.

Zaccheus of Hawke had a relative whose name was also Zaccheus, who was born in Poplin (modern-day Fremont) and was the son of yet a third Zaccheus Clough, tavern owner in Poplin and head of one of the wealthiest families in town. Since two of these three had died by 1790, it is not difficult to tell whether Primus Lane's first owner was Zaccheus the tavern owner, his son, or Zaccheus the blacksmith. Since Primus was owned by Enoch Coffin by 1790, the slave still owned by Zaccheus the blacksmith is unknown.

Primus enlisted in the Continental service, experiencing some of the most difficult engagements of the war. While on furlough in May of 1779 Primus married "Cill" Clough of Exeter. Both were listed as "Negro." After the marriage, Primus began calling himself Prince Lane rather than Primus Coffin.[89]

After the war, Primus was involved in two legal actions as recorded by the Rockingham County Court. The first involved an award of twenty pounds to Primus from Jonathan Greeley of Kingston for ninety days of work Primus had done for Greeley. The work included "the spinning of 34 seains of yarn, one pair of woman's stockings and for watching cattle one night."[90]

The second judgment of the court went against Primus. He lost the sum of eighteen pounds, nearly all that had been awarded earlier. Primus had failed to pay Dr. Tilton, who had provided "sundry medicines and attendance from February 7, 1780, to July 5, 1781, for him and his wife inclusively" and had not been paid.[91] Perhaps Primus was in need of money to pay for this fee, or just needed a reason not to be in Kingston for a time. In any case, he re-enlisted in 1782, this time for East Kingston. While he was away, his wife received welfare from the town. When Primus returned, he took up farming. He applied for a pension, which didn't begin until he was about eighty years old and was living in Deerfield, New Hampshire. Daniel Gookin was one of those who wrote testimony for Primus's pension application and stated that Primus had been his waiter for some of the duration of his enlistment. At the time Primus began to receive his pension in 1820, he does not seem to be living with any of his family. Little else is known about Primus.[92]

Plato Coleman

Plato Coleman was a black man who mustered in at Kingston, but hailed from Newington where he'd been a slave of James Coleman. He most likely could not write since he signed his name only with an *X*. He enlisted voluntarily and served at West Point. His name appears on a list of rations given out (rum, sugar, etc.), and he was also listed as sick. Plato ended his term of service in 1780 when he was discharged with none of the money he was due, excepting his blanket allowance and a little travel money. It appears that the town of Newington received his payment but Plato returned neither to Newington or Kingston.[93]

Enoch Greele

Enoch Greele is the last soldier from New Hampshire who enlisted in 1775 and served in Captain Philip Tilton's company. At the time he enlisted, Enoch claimed he was twenty-one and a resident farmer in Kingston. An Enoch Greele appears in Rumney in the 1800 New Hampshire Census as a "non-white" head of household with a white woman who was listed as forty-five years of age. In the 1810 census, the spelling of Enoch's name has become Greely. There is some evidence that after 1810, he moved to Hallowell, Maine, where he died.[94]

Caesar and Cato (Stevens/Black), Dinah Black

Caesar and Cato were slaves of the Ebenezer Stevens family of Kingston. Major Ebenezer Stevens married Elizabeth Colcord, and when he died in 1746, an account of his will states, "I give to Elizabeth, my beloved wife, my Negro servant Cato."[95] This is the last we hear of Cato as a slave in the Stevens family.

Ebenezer was characterized as "a very useful citizen and such was his integrity and benevolence that differences among people were submitted to his decision with perfect confidence."[96] Major Ebenezer Stevens was one of the original grantees of Kingston and saw action in the French and Indian War. One of his sons, Colonel Ebenezer Stevens, was born in 1715. When Colonel Ebenezer was seven years old, he was taken by the Indians into captivity and was rescued by his father. In 1749 Colonel Stevens received a Masonian land grant called Bakerstown. He died shortly after when the settlement was renamed Stevenstown, after Colonel Ebenezer. The colonel's son, Captain Ebenezer Jr. was born in 1739 and married Sarah Emerson. He, like his father, was a deacon in the Kingston church and it is likely that it is with this "Captain Ebenezer" that Caesar Stevens (Black) resided.

According to the Kingston town records, Caesar was born on August 17, 1754. These same records state that Dinah Black was born in 1752, and both Dinah and Caesar were owned by Captain Ebenezer Stevens. One wonders if Captain Ebenezer ever thought about the experience of his father's captivity by the Indians in relation to his own ownership of Caesar and Dinah. His ownership essentially made Caesar and Dinah his captives.

Caesar and Dinah were owned, however, even before they came to live with Ebenezer. They were bought at different times by Andrew McMillan. Benjamin Osgood sold Caesar, his boy slave, to Mr. McMillan in 1767, and, in 1768, Mr. McMillan bought of Patrick Gault a slave girl, aged, eight years, named Dinah. Caesar's and Dinah's bills of sale read as follows:

> Received of Andrew McMillan the sum of forty-seven pounds ten shillings, lawful money, in full consideration for my Negro Boy slave named Caesar, aged about eleven years, which Negro Boy I have this day sold to said McMillan, and promise to warrant and defend the property of said Negro Boy to him, the said McMillan, and his heirs or assigns forever, against the claims of any other person or persons whatsoever.
>
> In witness whereof I have hereunto set my hand and seal, the day and date - Concord, March 4, 1767. Benjamin Osgood.[97]
>
> Know all Men by these Presents, That I, Patrick Gault, of Chester, in His Majesty's Province of New-Hampshire, in New-England, husbandman, for and in consideration of the sum of twenty pounds, lawful money, to me in hand before the delivery hereof, well and truly paid by Andrew McMillan, of Concord, in the Province aforesaid, Esq., the receipt whereof I do hereby acknowledge, have bargained and sold, and by these presents do bargain and sell unto him, the said Andrew McMillan, my Negro Garl, named Dinah, aged about eight years, to have and to hold his said Negro Garl Dinah, by these presents, to him the said Andrew McMillan, his heirs, administrators and assigns; and I the said Patrick Gault, for myself, my heirs and administrators, shall and will warrant, and forever defend her, the said Negro Garl, unto him, the said Andrew McMillan, his heirs, administrators and assigns, against all the claims and demands of any person or persons whomsoever; and

have put her, the said Negro Garl, into his, the said Andrew McMillan's possession, by delivering her unto him, the said McMillan, at the time of sealing hereof. In witness whereof I have hereunto set my hand and seal, the 24th day of May and in the eighth year of His Majesty's reign, A.D. One thousand seven hundred and sixty-eight. Patrick Gault X

Caesar enlisted in the Continental service in 1777. In his early soldiering years, he went by Caesar Stevens. Later, however, he re-enlisted as Caesar Black, "from the parish of Sandown."[98] If Caesar and Dinah were related, it may have been as brother and sister, or as husband and wife. The records of Kingston do not include a record of their marriage. After the war, as late as 1799, there is a record of Caesar being warned out of Kingston and East Kingston. The record clearly states that Caesar was formerly owned by Ebenezer Stevens, so he has by this date exchanged his enslavement for impoverishment:

> TO: Oliver Welch, Constable of Kingston – warn Caesar, a Negro man formerly owned by Ebenezer Stevens to depart out of town. 1799

> To: Jacob Graves, Constable of E. Kingston – warn Josiah Sargent and Caesar Stevens, a black man, now residing in this town. 1799[99]

There is no mention of Dinah Black's death but Caesar Black lived until the age of ninety-two and died in Concord, New Hampshire.

Pompey (Hook)

Pompey was owned by Jacob Hook, one of the founding fathers of Kingston, who was also an owner of Prince Batchelder for a time. In 1777 Jacob's daughter, Mary, married Rev. Joseph

Appleton of Ipswich, Massachusetts. Rev. Appleton and Mary Hook Appleton had a son, William, who became a noted merchant and member of Congress. In one of William's diaries, he shares this recollection of his grandfather and his slave, Pompey: "He visited his widowed daughter, coming on horseback, followed by his faithful slave Pompey. He was a fine figure with queue and short clothes and ruff."[100] Jacob and Pompey must have visited with Mary after 1795, the year her husband Joseph died. There seems to be no other references to Pompey in any church or town records.

African Americans from the Granddaughter Church at Sandown, Incorporated 1756

Sandown, like Hawke, was a "spin-off" parish of Kingston. Moses Tucker, Israel and James Huse, James Graves, Thomas Wells and others were the first to settle there in 1736. Another twenty years would pass before the town was officially incorporated. One of the first acts of the town leaders was to call Rev. Josiah Cotton of Boston, the great-great-grandson of Rev. John Cotton, as the first pastor of the church. Rev. Cotton served in Sandown until 1780. The Congregational Society of Sandown ceased to exist in 1800.

None of the persons listed below is in the church record, however some unnamed African Americans are mentioned in the history of Sandown, including slaves owned at the time of Sandown's incorporation by Colonel Ebenezer Stevens. Also, Elizabeth Huntington had a servant maid named Elenor who was baptized in 1772. There is no indication that Elenor was of African origin. But, the names of three African Americans stand out in the town records of Sandown; those of Robin Negro, Thomas Griffin, and Ichabod Twilight.

Robin Negro (Rowell)

As the Revolutionary War became more and more a reality, towns were being asked to recruit soldiers. Sandown was having trouble making their quota of recruits and Thomas Rowell thought he knew how to solve this problem, at least for himself. He asked Robin Negro, his slave, to serve in his place. Robin was twenty-three years old at the time and enlisted in Capt. Jeremiah Gilman's Company for the town of Sandown, seeing action outside Boston, Massachusetts. Robin, a short time later, tried to enlist as a farmer with the consent of his master and tried joining a New Hampshire regiment at the same time as two other Negroes, Sippio and Archelaus (probably Archelaus White whose story appears under the Hampton section), from Plaistow. All three men were originally rejected, possibly because of an old law forbidding the service of slaves. One imagines that their reasoning was that they might be able to serve in a New Hampshire regiment stationed closer to home than Boston. Not much is known about Robin Negro other than his military service, but records show that even as late as 1782, Thomas Rowell was still receiving a tax rebate because of Robin's service in the military.[101]

Caesar Black (see more about Caesar Black under Kingston) also fought for Sandown under the leadership of Captain Caleb Robinson.

Ichabod Twilight

Ichabod was born in Boston in 1756. Since recruitment was also challenging in Massachusetts, Ichabod, variously described as both mulatto and "coloured," was approached and offered bounty money by the town of Newbury if he would fight in someone else's place. He took the money, but rather than enlist for Massachusetts, he proceeded north, maybe on his way to

Vermont, which was one of the earliest states to abolish slavery. As a free man, he found a place to settle in the town of Warner, New Hampshire, and from there was hired by Sandown in 1782. He fought in the 2nd New Hampshire Regiment under Captain Jeremiah Fogg. His service was brief.

After the war, Ichabod found his way through New York State to eventually settle in Cornish, Vermont. In 1789, he and his wife Mary began a family. Their first son Alexander, although indentured as a young man, was the first black man to ever graduate from an American college, that is, Middlebury, in 1823. He was also the first African American to ever be elected to the state legislature, in 1836. If this were not enough firsts, Alexander also married a white woman, Mercy Ladd Merrill, and taught for a few years in Vergennes, Vermont, before he served as a Congregational pastor in at least two Vermont parishes.

Ichabod's son William was a wanderer like his father. He lived for a time in Exeter, New Hampshire, describing himself as a farmer. He married and moved to Hampton where he was an innkeeper for a time before moving back to Exeter. From the 1850 census that names William, his family, and neighbors, it appears that he may have been innkeeper at the Railroad House, which sat on the site of the former Dearborn Inn and Leavitt Tavern. It is difficult to determine how long William was innkeeper at Hampton, but he had certainly moved back to Exeter before the inn was renamed as the Union House in 1860, when William and his family are listed as residents of Exeter. William's oldest son William Henry attended Phillips Exeter Academy and served in the Civil War. In an ironic twist, William Henry served in the same regiment, the 2nd New Hampshire, as had his grandfather, Ichabod. The Hampton list of deaths includes this account: "William Twilight's child died December 19, 1850."[102]

This account does not give the name of William's child

who died during William Twilight's sojourn to Hampton. William's occupation as innkeeper certainly represents a change in the roles available for an African American. One would like to imagine this is due to wider acceptance of leadership roles for African Americans by the mid-nineteenth century, which may be true, in part. However, in many historical references to the Twilight family, the remark was often made that they were of such light skin color that they often passed for white men and women.

Thomas Griffin and Ann Beck Griffin

Thomas Griffin was also listed as a resident of Sandown, New Hampshire. He married Ann Beck in 1775, and Rev. Josiah Cotton officiated at their marriage. Shortly after the wedding, Thomas enlisted for Massachusetts as a drummer and fifer. He saw service during the siege of Boston and later was stationed at Fort Ticonderoga. In 1778, he enlisted again, this time for the town of Salisbury, Massachusetts, after serving two short stints for New Hampshire. He had garrison duty near West Point. While Thomas was serving in the military, it is believed that Ann became friends with another Sandown resident, Mary Bailey. Mary and her husband Joseph were denied access to his pension because Joseph served less than six months.

When Thomas returned, he and Ann moved to Chester. In the 1810 census they were listed as free, non-white residents. In 1818 Thomas received his pension. He died in 1819, however, so he saw little compensation for his several years of service. The Griffins had a son, name unknown, and a daughter named Nancy. Ann raised both children in Chester for a number of years until after Nancy married, at which time, Ann moved to Concord to live with her daughter, whose married name was Morrill. With the help of a Concord lawyer named Franklin Pierce, Ann was able to receive some of Thomas's pension, beginning in 1838.[103]

African Americans from the Granddaughter Church at Danville (or Hawke)

Danville was a parish of Kingston. The first settlements were made by Jonathan Sanborn, Jacob Hook and others, between 1735 and 1739. It would be more than twenty years, in 1760, before it would be chartered as Hawke, in honor of Admiral Sir Edward Hawke. The town was renamed and incorporated as Danville in 1836. In the mid-eighteenth century, the first meeting house was built and used for the purpose of worship until about 1830. After that, a Baptist church drew off enough members so the building was largely unused, although it still stands today as a fine example of early meeting house architecture.

Prince Batchelder (Batchelder/Hook)

Although the 1775 census shows no Negroes or slaves for life listed as residents of the town of Hawke, there is one Negro servant, with ties to Hawke and East Kingston, who belonged to the Hook family in 1773. Jacob Hook, one of the founders of Hawke, had several children. One son, Jacob Hook Jr., received a Negro servant named Prince from his maternal Batchelder kinsmen.

Prince Batchelder had been a slave of Josiah Batchelder, husbandman of East Kingston and descendant of Rev. Stephen Batchelder, first pastor of the Hampton Church. Prince was given to Josiah's wife, Sarah (Page), in his will, dated 1760, along with his Pew in the East Parish meetinghouse. The will expressly names Josiah's "Negro Man Prince (by name)" and invites Sarah to "do with him as she pleaseth."[104]

She kept Prince for a time, as in 1761 he was listed as

taxable property owned by Josiah. At some time between 1761
and 1773, Prince was sold by Sarah Batchelder to Jacob Hook
or his son Jacob. Apparently, Prince could not abide his new
owner and ran away. This ad for his return was published in the
Boston Gazette:

> Ran away on the Evening of the 27th Instant
> from the Subscriber Jacob Hook of Hawke, in the
> County of Rockingham, Esq: a NEGRO MAN
> Servant named Prince, about 24 Years of age, five
> feet seven inches high, a think stocky Fellow, has a
> Scar in his Forehead near an Inch long, very crooked
> Legs and large Feet; was born in Boston, and Speaks
> English very well; carried off with him two home
> made Olive colour'd Coats and a Bengal one, a green
> Tarrien Jacket and a pair of striped Trewsers, and a
> new Felt Hat (which it is supposed he had on) and a
> large Quantity of other Cloaths, which mush make a
> large Pack. Whoever shall take up said NEGRO, and
> coney him to his said Master, shall have Five Dollars
> Reward and all necessary Charges paid by JACOB
> HOOK. N.B.
>
> All Masters of Vessels and Others, are cautioned
> against concealing or carrying him off. Hawke Sep
> 29, 1773. [105]

Prince was successful in gaining his freedom for a time, but in
1776 he joined the army at the same time that Josiah Batchelder, his first owner from East Kingston, joined. Prince and
Josiah served in Captain Simon Marston's company in Colonel
John Waldron's 18th Militia Regiment. One wonders if Prince
spent time as a run-away doing a lot of walking, because Simon
Marston marched his men, ninety miles to Winter Hill where
they served in the siege of Boston.[106] This service ended in April

of 1776 and there is a Prince Batchelder, born in 1750, who served for Massachusetts out of Amesbury as a private in the Revolutionary War, beginning in April. This Prince reported on command at Fort Ticonderoga until December when he enlisted again. Continental pay accounts detail Prince's service from January 1, 1777, to February 1778, when it was reported that he died. It is likely that this second Prince is the same person owned by Josiah Batchelder and Jacob Hook.

It is not unreasonable to find but one African American listed as having a connection to Hawke. It was a small town and by the late eighteenth century, the Revolutionary War was on the horizon. The war changed the perceptions held by many about the freedoms that must be afforded to all persons, especially those who had served as enslaved persons, in order that the emerging nation might be free to govern itself. In the years following the war, the numbers of Negro slaves held by slave owners in New Hampshire dropped precipitously.

What Do These Stories Tell Us?

W E END OUR LOOK at the daughter and grand-daughter churches of First Congregational Church of Hampton with a review of Prince Batchelder's story. He was owned by a family who resided in Hawke, the last granddaughter church descended from First Church in Hampton. He was owned by family who were descendants of Stephen Batchelder, who played a major role in the founding of First Congregational Church of Hampton, where our story began. We have come full circle.

We have discovered some of the several African American members of the First Congregational Church and its daughter and granddaughter churches who contributed in significant ways to the life of their parishes and towns. Doctors, merchants, ship owners, clergy, and landholders of large tracts of land were, in large measure, the slave owners, not just in Hampton but in every settlement that was established from Hampton's original boundaries. As the slave owners' businesses prospered and grew, the family slave became crucial not only to the work within the household, but also to the growth in trade and the establishing of businesses in each town. The town of Hampton could not have tended its sick without young slaves like Jock, Flora, Simon, or Caesar Long. Clergymen could not have traveled to ordinations nor could politicians have entertained the conversations of townsfolk at the tavern without slaves such as Sippio, Jenny, the unnamed black man and woman who worked for Rachel Freese, or Philip Burdoo, who worked in the Leavitt-Dearborn Tavern. The Toppan and Hussey families might never have been such successful merchants had they not had deck hands, farm hands, and house servants who kept their estates running through long absences, inclement weather, intermittent Indian attacks, or diseases such as the throat distemper, and the unpredictability of the hunt for fortune.

During roughly one hundred years of Hampton's history, between 1720 and 1820, the Hampton church records make distinct mention of African Americans as participating in the sacrament of baptism or becoming members by owning the covenant. During this same time span we can calculate that the percentage of the whole church membership which was African American, whether slave or free, who either joined the church or were baptized in the church. At its height about 4% of the total membership was African American. Between 1727 and 1759, due to two revivals, the total number of members increased by about 100, from 220 to 313 members. This thirty-year span also saw the highest number of African American members.

Rev. Ward Cotton was pastor at the time, and the First Great Awakening was underway during the early part of this era. Beginning in 1730 and continuing for about fifteen years, this revival movement was a powerful engine that drove people toward the meeting house door in search of the Spirit-filled life of joy that Rev. Whitefield, the traveling evangelist, proclaimed. Then, just as the steam from the first revival movement was dissipating, a Second Great Awakening was born and with it came a second wave of new members, along with an increase in the number of African American members—as many as fifteen out of three hundred. This may not seem significant until we compare this number with some of the Protestant churches throughout Massachusetts, even those in the heart of the city of Boston, which had a significant black population. Many such churches were rarely higher than 4% African American. This percentage is especially revealing when compared with the current percentage of African Americans members tallied in the 375th year of the Hampton church's founding. That percentage is calculated at less than 1%.

We may never be certain whether this relatively high percentage of African Americans was due to the more emotional style of preaching evidenced by the preachers of the Great Awakening; by the economic forces that conspired to create a boon in the merchant economy, or whether Rev. Ward Cotton was, himself, a welcoming and accessible pastor who encouraged the progress of the spiritual life of whites and blacks with equal enthusiasm. In truth, all of these realities may have played a role in encouraging more African Americans to join. Perhaps Rev. Cotton spent less of his time primarily reading and writing sermons? Maybe he visited in people's homes, helped nurse them when they were sick or dying, and encouraged their progress toward learning how to read and write? Statistics reveal that a more pastoral as opposed to a scholarly approach toward ministry does create a more welcoming and tolerant atmosphere within a faith community. Did this make a difference to some of the early African American members in their sense of belonging?

Some authors are beginning to wonder if the engagement of African Americans with Puritan ideas and practices was indirectly formative in the decline of slave-holding and the eventual abolition of slavery. The premise is this: slaves learned from watching their Puritan masters and then took initiatives toward gaining their freedom using what they had learned. For example, Thomas Choate owned a slave named Flora. She was one of many during the Great Awakening who was determined to give testimony before the members of the Congregational Church of Chebacco where she attended worship. She had heard Thomas witness and wanted her confession to also be her route to membership. She spoke eloquently about how she felt God had brought her soul from sin to grace through prayer.[1] She used the notion of the covenant that God makes with all of God's children to emphasize her surprise, astonishment and relief at realizing that God had included her in this covenant of grace. She was building the idea of equal grace under the covenant—a deeply Puritan belief and practice!

Other slaves went even further than Flora with the notion of covenant, and began to press the idea that slaveholders could not fully claim their status in the covenant as long as they were still oppressing their slaves. Their full blessing was denied until they relieved the slave's groaning in order that all might know Flora's 'astonishment' at inclusion. This oratory mimicked the style of Puritan preaching called "jeremiad" which is a sermon form that ties together social critique and spiritual renewal. It was meant to reinforce the notion that God was intimately concerned with the rightness of relationships and the peace of all of God's sons and daughters with the rest of creation.

Beyond Puritan concepts, even accepted Puritan practices such as believing any grievance could be taken before a group of peers and adjudicated with reason, law and sometimes even mercy may have played a role in abolishing slavery. Perhaps this was what Caesar Hendricks thought when he brought his wrongful enslavement question before the court and won. This Puritan practice of petitioning for change was used to good effect by Prince Whipple and others when they petitioned the New Hampshire legislature for their freedom. We tend to forget the power of such heady political practices and how this power must have been a fresh wind of hope for those bearing the weight of enslavement. We also tend to forget the effort it took to discover such inspiration when it might lie buried deep inside a two-hour sermon that touched more often on the fires of hell than the astonishment of graceful inclusion. Hell was a topic not infrequently employed against any notions of disobedience. Thus it was that the spiritual fires of the Great Awakening became smoldering ash.

By about 1755 and continuing up to the Revolutionary War, the number of African Americans choosing to become members of churches as well as those requesting baptism had begun to decline slightly. It is not certain what contributed to this decline, but it occurred in the after-glow of the revival movements. Rev. Ward Cotton had died, the number of new Congregational Churches that First Congregational Church had given birth to was established and a relatively flat period of growth in membership ensued in the run-up to the Revolution. One wonders if blacks began to realize that although welcome, they were not going to be given places of leadership in the Congregational faith community. Perhaps with the rise of other denominations—Methodist, Episcopal, and Baptist—African Americans were being more enthusiastically welcomed in the newer denominations, so their loss to the Congregational Church served simply to broaden the sense of interracial worship in other denominational churches in the community. These new denominations that were forming in Hampton and the wider area were faith communities who were less strict and less interested in frightening people into being good with the concept of hell. Worship was not so much an occasion to be taught as it was an occasion to be caught by the Holy Spirit. A worship hour that was filled with more music, more story-telling, and more encouragement toward living with a heart "strangely warmed" would have been a welcomed change to those who had a native faith that was expressed in clapping, drumming, singing, and witnessing with joy.

In the state of Pennsylvania, there was a significant number of Moravian Brethren communities, unlike Hampton where there were none. Moravian Brethren were less likely to have a high percentage of blacks who joined the churches and were less influenced by the theological ideas of the Great Awakening. One black, however, whose name was Andrew, kept a diary of his experiences in a Moravian church community. He wanted to give evidence of how earnestly and hopefully the Moravians tended to his soul and how their simple lifestyle made word and deed come together as an inspiration for him. Andrew says, "[T]hey [the Moravian Brethren] often told me that our Savior had shed his blood for me and all black men and that He had as much love for me, and everyone, as for white people, which I did not believe. On the contrary, I thought that God only loved people who were important in the world, who possessed riches, and so forth."[2] For Andrew, it took several Moravian brothers to convince him, by living their lives with integrity, that they meant what the said. It was their sincerity of word and deed, not their theology that helped Andrew know that as an African American he was welcome in the house of God.

This welcome does seem to have been genuine from the scant notes that are contained in the Hampton Church records. The pastor's notes reveal the intention of Hampton Church members, including those who owned slaves, to share their faith and the good news of salvation in Christ with their fellow members and slaves. Spiritual discipline could, however, become moral obedience under the strict teachings of certain of the Congregational pastors. Contained in St. Paul's letter to the Ephesians, we read, "Slaves, be obedient to those who are your earthly masters." We may never know the number of times that this passage from Ephesians was preached or taught as a way of maintaining the balance of power between slave and slave-owner.

However, in a closer reading of St. Paul, one might find him more subversive than imagined. If one reads this quote in context, we see that Paul is speaking directly to three subordinate categories of persons in his day—the wife, the child, and the slave. He is urging wife, child, and slave to be obedient not to please husband, parent or master, but as a means of obeying Christ. Those who do good for Christ's sake, he says, receive the same from the Lord, "whether slave or free." Since "in heaven there is no partiality with Him," Paul was telling these subordinate groups, speaking directly to them, and saying that they were as equals in God's eyes. Was this interpretation ever preached to the slave balconies, the women's section or to the children's pew?

While preaching obedience, both clergy and slave owners, in most cases, took care to grant to their slaves the rudimentary skills required to read and write. In many cases, this resulted in slaves such as Dinah Burdoo and Alice Page being praised for their faithfulness and progress toward becoming divine professors of the faith. Women such as Dinah Whipple and Phillis Parsons were able to use their education to become teachers of other African American children. However, as close as these black men and women got to mastering the same skills and proficiencies of their owners, the more certain these very same slave owners remained that their slave was still "other." God may have held no partiality, but human beings did and, unfortunately, still do.

Dinah Burdoo, Alice Page, and Phillis White were the last African American slaves (or former slaves) to die in Hampton, in 1826 and 1830 respectively. They died having received the care of church deacons and monies from discretionary charitable funds. Both Alice and Dinah received short eulogies from the pastor in the church record books, and the White family was given a burial place by Aiken Coffin. Dinah and Phillis saw their husbands and children go to war and, in many cases, come back unscathed. Phillis pleaded her case for receipt of her husband's pension with dignity and simple, truthful, eloquence. I imagine them as good-hearted women, like so many of the African-American men and women who lived and loved, lost and strove in the town of Hampton and its descendant towns. I'd like to believe that they yearned for God's love and the respect of their neighbors and in some measure received both, not in spite of the color of their skin, but because of the depth of their faith, the courage of their hearts and the "authority of the shepherd within."

Many in the Puritan Church believed that all persons of faith journeyed home to the shepherd Christ at their death. In this work, I have attempted to intermingle the experiences of African Americans with their European brothers and sisters in life and in death, so that their common journey of prayer and work is made visible. We do not just remember them, but, with the added color, texture, and vibrancy of their stories included, the whole history of the beloved faith communities of First Congregational Church of Hampton, her daughters and grand-daughters, becomes more dimensional and perhaps more true. There will always be a next step in the journey toward unity. This work has taught me that an eighteenth-century clergyman could describe an African American slave as "being well on [her] way to becoming a divine professor" and that same clergyman might not think twice about her being seated in the back pews or balcony pews, as far away from the more notable members of the faith community as she could be. Or, in other words, a slave could take on the name of Christ and be known as a child of God but even as such she or he might still have lived as bound or bent over in spirit. Only when all of us can journey with upright spirits and spines, when each one is able to walk in the shoes of the "other," can we honestly say that we are all colored "included." To that day!

Endnotes

Chapter 1 Notes

1. Julius Lester, *To Be a Slave* (New York: Puffin Publishing, 1998).

2. *Calendar of state papers, Colonial Series, America & West Indies, 1677–1680*, vol. 44, no. 61, (London: Gr. Britain Public Record Office, 1896), 529–530.

3. Joshua Coffin, *History of Newbury, Newburyport, and West Newbury from 1635–1845*, (Boston: Samuel G. Drake, 1845), 154.

4. Samuel Sewall, *The Selling of Joseph: A Memorial* (Boston: Green and Allen, 1700).

5. Elihu Coleman, *The Tract on Slavery* (Nantucket, 1729).

6. Acts and Laws Passed by the General Court of Assembly of His Majesty's Province of New Hampshire in New England, (Boston in New England: Printed by B. Green: sold by Eleazar Russel at his shop in Portsmouth, 1716–26); (original from British Library, digitized October 10, 2014), 36 and 48.

7. Felix (last name unknown), *Slave Petition for Freedom* (January 6, 1773). Quoted in Howard Zinn and Anthony Arnove, *Voices of a People's History of the United States* (New York: Seven Stories Press, 2004), 54.

8. Lorenzo Greene, *The Negro in Colonial New England 1629–1776* (Washington, NY: Kennikat Press, 1942), 74.

9. Joseph Dow, *History of the Town of Hampton from its Settlement in 1638 to the Autumn of 1892*, (Salem, MA: Salem Press Publishing and Printing Co., 1893), 268.

10. Rockingham County New Hampshire 1790 Census/1840 Census – Families with non-white members, www.rays-place.com/census/rockingham-city-nh.htm (accessed September 2013).

11. *New Hampshire Provincial and State Papers*, vol. 4, edited by Nathaniel Bouton, D. D., (Manchester, NH: John B. Clarke, printer, 1870), 305, 497, 499.

12. Lorenca Consuelo Rosal, *God Save the People: A New Hampshire History*, (Orford, NH: Equity Publishing Company, 1988), 70.

13. Ruth Wallis Herndon, To Live in the Manner of an Apprentice: Public Indenture and Social Control in Rhode Island, 1750–1800, (paper presented at the Annual Meeting of the American Studies Association, Boston, Massachusetts, November 7, 1993), 3, as quoted in Joanne Pope Melish, *Disowning Slavery: Gradual Emancipation and "Race" in New England, 1780-1860* (Ithaca: Cornell University Press, 1998), 100.

14. Joanne Pope Melish, *Disowning Slavery: Gradual Emancipation and "Race" in New England, 1780-1860*, (Ithica: Cornell University Press, 1998), 78.

Chapter 2 Notes

1. Genesis 17:1-8.

2. Exodus 19:1-37.

3. Alice Moise Earle, *The Sabbath in Puritan New England*, (Williamstown, MA: Corner House Publishing, 1974), 67.

4. Hughes Oliphant Old, *Moderation, Pietism and Awakening*, vol. 5 of *The Reading and Preaching of the Scriptures in the Worship of the Christian Church* (Grand Rapids, MI: Wm E. Eerdmans Publishing Co., 2004), 207.

5. Jeffrey Benner, "Translating the Word 'lev'." Ancient Hebrew Research Center http://www.ancient-hebrew.org/27_heart.html (accessed October 2013).

6. Richard J. Boles, "Dividing the Faith: The Rise of Racially Segregated Northern Churches, 1730-1850" (Ph.D dissertation, The Colombian College of Arts and Sciences, George Washington University, May 19, 2013), (accessed through Proquest LLC., 2013), viii. Proquest is a service that places digitized versions of dissertations on-line.

Chapter 3 Notes

1. Records and Files of the Quarterly Courts of Essex County, Massachusetts, vol. 4, 1667–1671 (Salem, MA: Essex Institute, 1914), 135.

2. Joseph Dow, 287.

3. "The Diary of Captain Henry Dow," 1672–1702, [diary photocopy], Hampton Historical Society Archives, Hampton, New Hampshire.

4. Ibid.

5. Sybil Noyes, Charles Thornton Libbey, Walter Goodwin Davis, *Genealogical Dictionary of Maine and New Hampshire,* (Portland, ME: Genealogical Publishing Company, 1939), 365.

6. Henry B. Worth, extracted from *Nantucket Lands and Land Owners,* "Wills and Estates," Chapter XIV (1680–1778), vol. 2, no. 6, (Nantucket Historical Society, 1901), 304–305. https://www.archive. org/stream/nantucketlandsla01wort/nantucketlandsla01wort_djvu.txt (accessed November 2013).

7. Noyes, Libbey, and Davis, 343–344.

8. Mildred Roth; of Mitchell, SD; a descendant of William Holdredge, reported in a message dated July 1993 to the Holdredge Family ancestor, Betty Brasington that she "looked for records of the trial of Negro Jack but found only the record of his imprisonment for four weeks for 'murthering the widow Isabell Holdredge'"; from Landon Family Research Quarterly, vol. 2, Issue 3, http://homepages. rootsweb.ancestry.com/~landon/1993_3/1993_3f.html (accessed November 2013).

9. Langdon Papers, Box 1, Folder 2, Series 2. Strawbery Banke Museum, Portsmouth, NH.

Chapter 4 Notes

1. *First Congregational Church Record Book,* vol. 2, 40.

2. *First Congregational Church Record Book,* vol. I & II, 118, (baptism), 172, (full communion).

3. Thomas E. Jones, *Captain Thomas Cromwell, 17th C Pirate* (Boston, MA: The New England Historic Genealogical Society, December 1985).

4. Noyes, Libbey, and Davis, 630.

5. Antonio T. Bly, ed., *Escaping Bondage: A Documentary History of Runaway Slaves in Eighteenth Century New England, 1700–1789* (Lanham, MD: Lexington Books, 2012), 86.

6. Joseph Dow, 189.

7. "Josiah Page's Journal of Epidemic Deaths, 1661–1856" (Hampton Historical Society Archives, 2009.087).

8. *First Congregational Church Record Book,* "Deaths," vol. I & II, 279.

9. *Probate Records of the Province of New Hampshire,* 1750-1753, vol. 34, 442–443. http://www.library.unh.edu/digital/object/propapers:0034 (Accessed from UNH Digital Collections, The New Hampshire History Bookshelf, October, 2014).

10. *First Congregational Church Record Book,* vol. I & II, "Baptisms," 190.

11. *Probate Records of the Province of New Hampshire,* 1718–1740, vol. 32, (Bristol, NH: R.W. Musgrove, 1914), 503.

12. *First Congregational Church Record Book,* vol. I & II, "Baptisms," 211.

13. John Slaughter, Founder, "The Massachusetts Vital Records Project 1620-1988, Nantucket marriages. Transcriptions of the published vital records of early Massachusetts towns from the "Tan Book" series. www.ma-vitalrecords.org/MA/Nantucket/Nantucket1 (accessed October 2014).

14. "U.S. Revolutionary War Pension & Bounty-Land Warrant Application Files 1800–1900," Archive Publication Number M804, Archive Roll Number 1085, 7 pages in packet, National Archives: Washington, D. C.; microfilm available through subscription to Ancestry.com.

15. *First Congregational Church Record Book,* vol. I & II, "Deaths," 282.

16. Helen Evans, *Abstracts of Probate Records of Rockingham County, New Hampshire, 1771–1799,* vol. 1, (Bowie, MD: Heritage Books, Inc., 2000), 408.

17. *First Congregational Church Record Book,* vol. 2, 142, 185.

18. Ibid., 235.

19. "Sarah Toppan's (Mrs. Christopher) Account Book, 1820–1826," (Tuck Museum, 2006.55), Hampton Historical Society, Hampton, NH.

20. Susannah J. Clark, Richard Curl, eds., *The Vital Records of North Hampton, New Hampshire,* (Melrose, MA: CV Publishing, 2009), 135.

21. Roland Page [?author], A List of Deaths in Hampton, New Hampshire, 1767–1875, an online record transcribed by Michael

Lane, 33. A photocopy of the original, handwritten list can be accessed at www.hampton.lib.nh.us/hampton/documents/deaths/index.htm, (accessed December 2014).

22. Juliet Haines Moffard, *The Devil Made Me Do It, Crime and Punishment in Early New England* (Guildford, CT: Globe Pequot Press, 2012), 79.

23. Clark & Curl, "Deaths," 135.

Chapter 5 Notes

1. George F. Shrady, Thomas L. Stedman, eds., "The Conduct of a Surgeon," *Medical Record*, vol. 35 (April 20, 1889), 438. A weekly Journal of Medicine and Surgery, New York: William Wood & Company, Trow's Printing and Bookbinding Co. EBook: https://books.google.com/books/abut/Medical_Record, html?id=8AZYAAAAYAAJ (accessed, June 2103).

2. *First Congregational Church Record Book,* vol. I & II, 198; also Joseph Dow, 399–401.

3. *First Congregational Church Record Book,* vol. I & II, 210.

4. Ibid, 284.

5. Joseph Dow, 287.

6. John Slaughter, Founder, *The Massachusetts Vital Records Project, Vital Records of Salisbury 1600-1850, Deaths, Baptisms, Marriages,* (2005), www.ma-vitalrecords.org/MA/Essex/Salisbury/ (accessed November, 2014).

7. *First Congregational Church Record Book,* vol. 2, 1.

8. *First Congregational Church Record Book,* vol. I & II, 210.

9. Joseph Dow, 399.

10. *Probate Records of the Province of New Hampshire,* vol. 7, 1760-1763, edited by Otis G. Hammond, (State of NH, 1939), 112.

11. Ibid, 33.

Chapter 6 Notes

1. *First Congregational Church Record Book,* vol. I & II, "Baptisms," 212.

2. "Town of North Hampton Time Line," North Hampton Heritage Commission, year 1776. On-line at: www.northhampton-nh.gov/

public_documents/NorthhamptonNH_BComm/heritage. A living document of chronologically listed facts about North Hampton, updated every six months. (accessed January 2014).

3. *Probate Records of the Province of New Hampshire*, vol. 5, 1754–1756, Edited by Otis G. Hammond, (State of NH, 1936), Joseph Whipple, 78.

4. "Joseph Whipple Diaries, 1731–1736," Accessed in Pre-Revolutionary Diaries Collection of Manuscripts, Massachusetts Historical Society, microfilm reel, 11.14-11.18, Boston, MA.

5. Glenn A. Knoblock, *Strong and Brave Fellows – New Hampshire's Black Soldiers and Sailors of the American Revolution, 1775–1784* (Jefferson, N.C. & London: McFarland & Company, Inc, 2003), 266.

6. New Hampshire Census Records, Town of Exeter, 1790, 1800. Also see Charles H. Bell, *History of the Town of Exeter, NH* (J.E. Farwell & Co., 1888), 266.

7. Portsmouth Town Records, vol. 2, 313.

8. *First Congregational Church Record Book,* vol. I & II, "Baptisms," 254.

9. Carol Hymowitz and Michaele Weissman, *History of Women in America* (New York: Bantam, 1978), 43.

10. Pauline Johnson Oesterlin, *Rockingham County, New Hampshire, Paupers*, Seabrook Warning Out #4241, (Berwyn Heights, MD: Heritage Books, Inc., 1992), 77. Entries in this volume are listed alphabetically by last name of persons who received support by towns or by the county. Actual record of "warning out" was issued by the Rockingham County Superior Court. Original loose documents at the New Hampshire State Archives, Concord.

11. *First Congregational Church Record Book,* vol. 2, "Deaths," 9, and Joseph Dow; 288.

12. *Probate Records of the Province of New Hampshire*, vol. 3, 1741–1749, Ed. By Henry Harrison Metcalf and Otis G. Hammond, (Concord, NH: The Rumford Press, 1915), 39–40.

13. Bly, 32.

14. Clark and Curl, 80 and 127.

15. *Published New Hampshire Revolutionary War Rolls*, vol. 1, Edited by Isaac Hammond, (Concord, N. H.: Parsons B. Cogswell, Sate Printer 1885), 351.

16. Knoblock, 140.

17. Ibid., 139.

18. *New Hampshire Provincial and State Papers*, vol. 12, Documents relating to Towns in New Hampshire, Gilmanton to New Ipswich, edited by Isaac W. Hammond, (Concord, N. H.: Parsons B. Cogswell, State Printer, 1883), 122–3.

19. Knoblock, 139.

20. *First Congregational Church Record Book*, vol. I & II, "Baptisms," 266, and vol. 2, "Deaths," 6.

21. *First Congregational Church Record Book*, vol. I & II, 270.

22. *First Congregational Church Record Book*, vol. 2, "Deaths," 10.

23. *North Hampton Church Records*, 27.

24. Clark and Curl, 123, 137.

25. *First Congregational Church Record*, vol. I & II, "Baptisms," 260.

26. William Haslet James, *Vital Statistics of North Hampton, New Hampshire, 1742–1942*, (Bowie, MD: Heritage Books, Inc., 1999), 250.

27. Clark and Curl, 54.

28. Langdon, B. Parsons, *The History of the Town of Rye, New Hampshire From its Discovery and Settlement to December 31, 1903* (Concord, NH: Rumford Printing Co., 1905), 212. Also in Bly,190–191.

29. Knoblock, 140–141. Also in James, *Vital Statistics of North Hampton*, 250.

30. Clark and Curl, 73.

31. U.S. Revolutionary War Pension and Bounty Land Warrant Application File, online data base, Archive Publishing Number, M804, Roll Number 1581m, 18 pages in packet; National Archives, Washington, D. C., microfilm available through subscription to: Ancestry.com,

32. "Town of North Hampton Time Line," North Hampton Heritage Commission, year 1823.

33. *First Congregational Church Record Book*, vol. 2, "Deaths," 205.

34. *Massachusetts Soldiers and Sailors of the Revolutionary War* (Boston, MA: Wright and Potter Printing, 1906). This publication is a compilation of archives.

35. Knoblock, 168.

36. Joseph Dow, 287.

37. Rockingham County Court Records, "Warning Out" 1774, Document #3061 for Cezar Small of Hampton. New Hampshire State Archives, Concord, N.H.

38. Joseph Dow, 287.

39. Mary Fuhrer, "Servitude and Slavery in 1775 Lexington," (Lexington: MA, 2012) One in a series of research papers published on behalf of The Lexington Historical Society, 140.

40. *First Congregational Church Record Book,* vol. 2, "Marriages," 266.

41. Joseph Dow, 287.

42. Digital copy of "Hampton, New Hampshire Town Records, 1798–1825," vol. 3, images 109–111, pages 210–214. Digital records can be accessed from the Hampton Historical Society website at general ledger entry for March 11, 1806.

43. Joseph Dow, 286–287.

44. *First Congregational Church Record Book,* vol. 2, "Deaths," 233.

45. Fuhrer, 142.

46. Lexington Historical Society Archives, Lexington, Mass., June 2, 1739; 1649 MSS in Ledgers: Book D, 61.

47. Kelly A. Ryan, *Regulating Passion Sexuality & Patriarchal Rule in Massachusetts, 1700-1830,* (New York: Oxford University Press, 2014), 227 endnotes.

48. Charles Hudson, *History of the Town of Lexington, Middlesex County, Massachusetts,* vol. 2, (Boston, MA: Houghton-Mifflin, 1913), 81 footnote.

49. May Grace Canfield, *The Valley of the Kedron: The Story of the South Parish, Woodstock, VT,* (South Woodstock, VT: Kedron Assoc., 1940), 245.

50. Knoblock, 254.

51. *New Hampshire Provincial and State Papers*, vol. 12, 303.

52. Rosal, 75.

53. Ibid.

54. Cambridge, Massachusetts, Vital Records to 1850, Marriages, (New England Genealogical Society, Boston, 1914).

55. *New Hampshire Gazette*, November 2, 1775, 1, and Knoblock, 154.

56. Bly, 192–193.

57. *Northwest Ordinance of 1787.*

58. "General Jonathan Moulton," by Sarah Hobbs Lane, ca. 1893, online, Lane Memorial Library, originally appeared in Fogg's *Gazette*, www. hamptonlib.nh.us/hampton/biog/mo (accessed October 2013).

59. *First Congregational Church Record Book,* vol. 2, 131.

60. Charles E. L. Wingate, ed., *Excerpts from the Life and Letters of Paine Wingate One of the Fathers of the Nation* (Medford, MA: James D.P. Wingate, 1930), 2.

61. Clark and Curl, 52 and 70.

62. Mark J. Sammons and Valerie Cunningham, *Black Portsmouth: Three Centuries of African-American Heritage* (Durham, NH: University of New Hampshire Press, 2004), 91.

63. Samuel Penhallow, *Collections Account Book*, 17th Century Materials, North Church Papers, MS036, Box 8, Folder 13, 1802–1821, Portsmouth Athenaeum.

64. *First Congregational Church Record Book,* vol. 3, 57.

65. Sammons and Cunningham, 116.

66. Joseph Dow, 288.

67. Lucy Ellen Dow, *An Historical Sketch of Hampton, N.H., 1638–1888*, online resource on the Lane Memorial Library Website, www. hampton.lib.nh.us/hampton/historyvignettes/lucydow.htm (accessed November 2014).

68. Joseph Dow, 288.

69. *First Congregational Church Record Book,* vol. 2, 241.

70. Joseph Dow, 288. Permission given for a walking of the parcel by current owner to search for topographical indication of these gravesites.

71. Knoblock, 242.

72. Rockingham County, New Hampshire, 1790 State Census, Families with Non-White Members, www.rays-place.com/census/rockingham-14.htm, (accessed September 9, 2013).

73. Knoblock, 242.

74. Oesterlin, Pauper List documents 20107 and 311.

75. U.S. Revolutionary War Pension and Bounty Land Warrant Application File, online data base, Pension #S43299, National Archives, Washington D. C., microfilm records available through subscription to Ancestry.com (accessed January 2014).

76. David T. Dixon, "Freedom Earned, Equality Denied: Evolving Race Relations in Exeter and Vicinity, 1776–1876," Printed in *Historical New Hampshire*, 61:1 (Spring 2007), 29–47.

Chapter 7 Notes

1. Rockingham County, New Hampshire, 1790 State Census, Families with non-white members, website: www.rays-place.com/census/rockingham-14.htm, (accessed September 9, 2013).

2. Dean Dudley, *History of the Dudley Family*, Number 1, (Montrose, MA: 1886), 242 and 244.

3. *Probate Records of the Province of New Hampshire*, vol. 2, 1718-1740, 183.

4. *First Congregational Church Record Book,* vol. I & II, "Baptisms," 192.

5. Knoblock, 95.

6. Bell, 58.

7. Rockingham County, New Hampshire, 1790 State Census, Families with non-white members (accessed September 2013).

8. Joseph Dow, 709.

9. Lane Memorial Library, Hampton, New Hampshire, Area Genealogy @ Rootsweb: Ancestry.com, contact: Richard Marston, wc.rootsweb.ancestry.com/cgi-bin/igm.cgi?db=Hampton-nh, copyright 1996–2011. A database for all residents of Hampton prior to 1900. Primary source, Joseph Dow's *History*, vol. 1–2, (accessed January 2014).

10. Brown, 571; Knoblock, 149; Hampton Falls Town Records, loose item.

11. Brown, 240.

12. *New Hampshire Provincial and State Papers*, vol. 18, ed. by Isaac W. Hammond, (Manchester, New Hampshire: John B. Clarke, 1890), 317–18.

13. Knoblock, 150.

14. Ibid.

15. *New Hampshire Revolutionary War Records*, vol. 1, ed. by Isaac W. Hammond, (Concord, N. H.: Parsons B. Cogswell, State Printer, 1885), 111.

16. Knoblock, 151.

17. Brown, 298.

18. Knoblock, 148.

19. Ibid.

20. Ibid., 149.

21. Ibid.

22. Ibid., 147.

23. Rockingham County, New Hampshire, State Census, 1790 State Census, Families with non-white members, website: www.rays-place.com/census/rockingham-14.htm, (accessed September 9, 2013).

24. Brown, 298.

25. Ibid., 614.

Chapter 8 Notes

1. Dalton Databank.org, "The First Daltons in the New World," www.daltondatabank.org/chronicles/first_Daltons_In_America.htm, (accessed September, 2013).

2. "Maine Will Abstracts for Residents of York County, Massachusetts, 1640–1760," Probate Office, 1, 69.

3. Ibid. 6, 206.

4. *Probate Records of the Province of New Hampshire*, vol. 9, Otis G. Hammond, ed., (State of New Hampshire 1941), 98; and Steve J. Plummer, *The Wheelright Family Story*, (Britain: Cloth Wrap Publishing, 2010), 168.

5. Dow, 385.

6. "Records of the Pine Grove Cemetery," Hampton, New Hampshire.

7. *First Congregational Church Record Book,* vol. I & II, "Baptisms and Deaths," 210, 294.

8. Rockingham County Court Records, "Warnings Out," 1781–1801, Documents #9740, 16050, 17750, 20206, Cato Fisk. New Hampshire State Archives, Concord, NH.

9. *First Congregational Church Record Book,* vol. 2, 223.

10. Noyes, Libbey, and Davis, 655.

11. Helen Evans, *Abstracts of the Probate Records of Rockingham County,* #4830 Captain Joseph Cilley, 1775.

12. *Granite Monthly New Hampshire Magazine,* vol. 2 (Concord: Granite Monthly Co., 1911), 206, and "Memoirs and Services of Three Generations of Cilleys," Reprint from the *Courier Gazette,* (Rockland, ME: 1909), 37.

13. Bell, 51.

14. John Longfellow Scales, "The Longfellow Garrison," *The DAR Magazine,* vol. 38:5, May 1911 (New York: National Society Of DAR), 246.

15. *Probate Records of the Province of New Hampshire,* vol. 2, 1718–1740, Henry Metcalf, ed., (Bristol, NH: R.W. Musgrove, 1914), 523.

16. Charles E. L. Wingate, *Life and Letters of Paine Wingate,* (Medford Massachusetts: The Mercury Printing Company, 1930), excerpts on-line at www.hampton.lib.nh.us/hampton/biog/wingatefamily.htm, (accessed April 2013).

17. Joshua Coffin, *A Sketch of Newbury, Newburyport and West Newbury 1635–1845* (Boston, MA: Samuel G. Drake, 1845), 339.

18. Chaim M. Rosenberg, *The Life and Times of Frances Cabot Lowell 1775–1817* (Lanham: MD, Lexington Books, 2011), 22–23.

19. Rockingham County Court Records, "Warning Out," 1794, Document 14018, Pomp Jackson. New Hampshire, State Archives, Concord, NH.

Chapter 9 Notes

1. *First Congregational Church Record Book,* vol. I & II, 15.

2. *The Universalist Society Church Records of Hampton Falls,* beginning January 2, 1712; entries by Theophilus Cotton, Pastor of that Church,

Baptism Record, June 14, 1713, 56. New Hampshire Historical Society, Tuck Library, Concord, NH.

3. Charles Wyllys Elliott, *The New England History: from the Discovery of the Continent by the Northmen, AD 1776,* (New York: Scribner, 1857), 181.

4. *The Universalist Society Church Records of Hampton Falls*, "Children and Other Persons Baptized by Joseph Whipple," 78.

5. Ibid., "Marriages," 36.

6. Ibid., "Baptism," 86; "Membership," 103.

7. Ibid, 78, 80.

8. Ibid., "Baptism," 88, 15; "Membership," 90.

9. Ibid., 89, 104.

10. *Probate Records of the Province of New Hampshire*, vol. 34, Otis G. Hammond, ed., (State of New Hampshire, 1933), 108.

11. Warren Brown, *The History of Hampton Falls, NH,* vol. 2, (Concord, NH: Rumford Press, 1918), 114.

12. *First Congregational Church Record Book,* vol. I & II, "Baptisms," 210.

13. *First Congregational Church Record Book,* vol. 2, 39.

14. Vital Records of South Hampton (Town Records), vol. 1, 256.

15. Bly, 126.

16. John Slaughter, founder, "The Massachusetts Vital Records Project, Vital Records of Salisbury, Massachusetts, 1600–1850, Deaths, Baptisms, Marriages," Transcriptions of the published vital records of early Massachusetts towns from the "Tan Book" series, www.mavitalrecords.org/MA/Essex/Salisbury/, (accessed November 2014).

17. Hamilton D. Hurd, *History of Rockingham and Strafford Counties, New Hampshire, with biographical sketches of many of its pioneers and prominent men*, Chapter 53, (Town of Kensington), (Philadelphia PA: J.W. Lewis and Co., 1882), 359.

18. Henry Parsons, A. M., "Descendants of Cornet Joseph Parsons, Springfield 1636-North Hampton 1655," vol. 2, (New Haven, CT: The Tuttle, Morehouse and Taylor Co., 1920), 13, www.archive.org/stream/parsonsfamilydes02pars#page/12/mode/2up/search/Negro (accessed June 2014).

19. Hurd, *History of Rockingham and Strafford Counties, New Hampshire*, 539.

20. Ibid.

21. Charles A. Hazlett, *History of Rockingham County, New Hampshire, and Representative Citizens* (Chicago, IL: Richmond-Arnold Publishing Co., 1915), 481.

22. John Slaughter, ed, The Massachusetts Vital Records Project from 1600–1850, "Vital Records of Salisbury, Massachusetts," copyright, 2005–2014, www.ma-vitalrecords.org/MA/Essex/Salisbury/. (accessed November 2014).

23. Joseph Merrill, *The History of Amesbury Including the first 17 Years of Salisbury to the Separation in 1654 and Merrimack from its Incorporation 1876* (Haverhill, MA: Press of Franklin P. Stiles, 1880), 297.

24. Knoblock, 283-4; Rockingham County Court Records, "Warnings Out," 1774–1780, #3061 and #4331, Ebenezer Mingo. NH State Archives, Concord, NH.

25. Essex County, Massachusetts, 1790 Census, Amesbury.

26. Sarah Cram, "Reminiscences of Hampton Falls, New Hampshire," *Exeter Newsletter*, 2 April 1826, as quoted in George Qunital, Jr., "Patriots of Color: A Peculiar Beauty and Merit," *African Americans and Native Americans at Battle Road & Bunker Hill*, (Boston, MA: National Park Service, 2002), 117, footnote 4.

27. Rev. Roland D. Sawyer, *The History of Kensington, NH 1663-1945*, (Farmington, ME: Knowlton and McLeary Co., 1946), 202.

28. Rockingham County Court Records, "Warning Out," 1787, Document #9740, Cato Fisk. NH State Archives, Concord, NH.

29. United States Revolutionary Pension and Bounty Land Warrant Application Files; National Archives: Washington, DC, microfilm available through subscription to Ancestry.com.

30. Erik R. Tuveson, "A People of Color: A Study of Race and Racial Identification in New Hampshire 1750–1825," (Master's thesis, University of New Hampshire, 1995), 28.

31. Ibid., 33.

32. Sawyer, 202.

33. Knoblock, 121.

34. Joseph Dow, 1030.

35. The Universalist Society Church Records of Hampton Falls, p. 86.

36. Rockingham County Court Records, "Warning Out," 1774, Document #3061, Timothy Nokes. NH State Archives, Concord, NH.

37. Knoblock, 221.

38. Clark and Curl, 52.

39. Ibid., 53.

40. *Probate Records of the Province of New Hampshire*, vol. 38, 308.

41. Clark and Curl, 54.

42. Ibid.

43. Ibid., 70, and "Town of North Hampton Time-line," North Hampton Heritage Commission, year 1779, www.northhampton-nh.gov/public_documents/NorthhamptonNH_Bcomm/Heritage, (accessed January 2015), A living document of chronologically listed facts about North Hampton, updated every six months.

44. Clark and Curl, 81.

45. *New Hampshire Gazette*, July 15, 1780, Portsmouth, NH.

46. Knoblock, 27, 43; Published State Records – New Hampshire Revolutionary War Records, vol. 1, ed. by Isaac W. Hammond, (Concord, NH: Parsons B. Cogswell, State Printer, 1885), 82, 198.

47. Eric G. Grundset, ed., *Forgotten Patriots—African American and Indian American Patriots of the Revolutionary War*, (National Society of DAR, online since 2008). Also found in *New Hampshire Gazette*, 28 April 1769, vol. 13, no. 655, 3, Portsmouth, NH. www.dar.org/sites/default/files/media/library/DARpublications/Forgotten_Patriots_ISBN-978-1-892237-10-1.pdf (Accessed November 2013).

48. *Probate Records of the Province of New Hampshire*, vol. 2, 357.

49. Bly, 88.

50. Louise H. Tallman, "Baptismal Records of Rye, New Hampshire, from the Congregational Records," (Rye, NH: 1980), New Hampshire Historical Society, Tuck Library Collection, Concord, NH [70] pages, typescript Xerox copy.

51. Langdon Brown Parsons, *History of the Town of Rye, New Hampshire From its Settlement to December 31, 1903* (Rye, NH: Rumford Printing, 1905), 212.

52. Tallman.

53. Parsons, 212.

54. Parsons, 583.

55. Parsons, 213.

56. Parsons, 212; and James Gray Garland, *Garland Genealogy – The Descendants of the Northern Branch of Peter Garland, Mariner* (Biddeford, ME: Watson's Illuminator Print, 1897), 24.

57. Lauren Landi, "Reading Between the Lines of Slavery: Examining New England Runaway Ads for Evidence of Afro-Yankee Culture," (Pell Scholar thesis, Salve Regina University; December 2, 2011).

58. Knoblock, 128, 136.

59. Parsons, 213.

60. Kathleen E. Hosier, *Vital Records of Rye, New Hampshire,* (Bowie, MD: Heritage Books, 1992), 141.

61. Parsons, 212.

62. Helen F. Evans, *Abstracts of the Probate Records of Rockingham County, NH, 1771–1799,* vol. 2, (Berwyn, MD: Heritage Books, 2000), 982.

63. Bly, 295.

64. Parsons, 212.

65. Rockingham County Court Records, "Warning Out," Document. Caesar Wallis. New Hampshire State Archives, Concord, NH.

66. Knoblock, 178-180.

67. Parsons, 212.

68. Knoblock, 182.

69. Parsons, 577.

70. Knoblock, 177. "North Church Records," Portsmouth, New Hampshire, vol. 1, 159. New Hampshire State Archives Office of Records Management, Concord.

71. *First Congregational Church Record Book,* vol. I & II, 113.

72. *Probate Records of the Province of New Hampshire,* vol. 2, 626.

73. "Kingston First Church Records," 1725–37, 8.

74. Ibid., 10.

75. George Thomas Little, ed., *Genealogical and Family History of the State of Maine*, vol. 2 (New York: Lewis Historical Publishing Co., 1909), https://archive.org/stream/genealogicalfam:001itt#page/707/mode/2up (accessed January 2015).

76. Church Records of Kingston, 2nd Parish, East Kingston, Baptisms, 14, 40, 302, 307, 308, 313.

77. 1790 Census data for Kingston, NH.

78. Charles Chase Lord, *Life and Times in Hopkinton, New Hampshire* (Concord, NH: Republica Press Assoc., 1890), 528–9.

79. Rockingham County Court Records, "Warning Out," Document #15598, Seco.

80. Rockingham County Records, Pauper Rolls and "Warning Out" Documents #430154, 440, Seco & Phillis.

81. Rockingham County Court Records, "Warning Out" Document, Doc# 311, Polly.

82. Knoblock, 86.

83. Knoblock, 27.

84. Rolls of Revolutionary War Soldiers, (May 1777–1780), ed. by Isaac W. Hammond, (Concord, NH: Parsons B. Cogswell, 1886), vol. 15:437.

85. Josiah Bartlett, *The Papers of Josiah Bartlett*, Frank C. Mevers, Ed. (Hanover, New Hampshire: University Press of New England 1979), 32. Publication of New Hampshire Historical Society, Concord, New Hampshire.

86. *Probate Records of the Province of New Hampshire*, vol.32, (Bristol, NH: R.W. Musgrove, 1914), 523–4.

87. Knoblock, 96.

88. Bell, 88.

89. Bell, 58; Knoblock, 96.

90. Rockingham County Court Records, Pauper Records #5054, Primus Coffin.

91. Rockingham County Court Records, Pauper Records #5070, Primus Coffin.

92. U.S. Revolutionary War Pension File, online data base, National Archives: Washington, D.C., Microfilm records available through subscription to Ancestry.com. (Accessed February 2015).

93. Knoblock, 99.

94. Knoblock, 117–118.

95. *Probate Records of the Province of New Hampshire* , vol. 3, 405.

96. Hamilton Hurd, *History of Rockingham and Strafford County*, 376.

97. Nathaniel Bouton, *The History of Concord From its First Grant in 1725 to the Organization of the City Grant in 1853* (Concord, NH: Benning W. Sanborn, 1856), 249–250.

98. New Hampshire Revolutionary War Records, vol. 3, 829-830.

99. Rockingham County Court Records, Pauper Records, #18299, Caesar Stevens.

100. William Appleton, *Selections from the Diaries of William Appleton 1786–1862*, (Boston, 1922), 94. 99. Rockingham County Court Records, Pauper Records, #18299, Caesar Stevens.

101. Knoblock, 228–229.

102. Knoblock, 238–240; A List of Deaths in Hampton 1767–1875, author unknown, a photocopy of the original handwritten list can be accessed at www.hampton.lib.nh.us/hampton/documents/deaths/index.htm. (Accessed December 2014).

103. Knoblock, 214-215.

104. *Probate Records of the Province of New Hampshire*, vol. 3, 38.

105. *Boston Gazette*, 8 November 1773, vol. 18, issue 885, Boston Massachusetts, 4.

106. Knoblock, 80.

Conclusion: What Do These Stories Tell Us?

1. Christopher Cameron, "The Puritan Origins of Black Abolitionists in Massachusetts," *The Historical Journal of Massachusetts*, vol. 39, (Summer 2011), 87.

2. Boles, 100.

Bibliography

Church Records

First Congregational Church Record Book, Volume I & II. Copied from original records, pp. 1–6; fragmentary records of Rev. Seaborn Cotton as copied by John Cotton, pp. 7–58; records of Rev. John Cotton, 1696–1710; pp. 60–173, records of Rev. Nathaniel Gookin, 1710–1734; pp. 174–300, a portion of records of Rev. Ward Cotton, 1765. Records are located at the First Congregational Church, in Hampton, NH, in the church's Archives. [Note: Refer to the Preface for a complete discussion of the church records references as Volumes I & II, Volume 2, and Volume 3.]

First Congregational Church Record Book, Volume 2. Containing the remaining records of Rev. Ward Cotton, pp., 1–84; records of Rev. Ebenezer Thayer, 1766–1792; records of Rev. Jesse Appleton, 1796–1807; and records of Rev. Josiah Webster, 1808–1837. Copied from original books, 2 and 3, located at the First Congregational Church, in Hampton, NH, in the church's Archives.

First Congregational Church Record Book, Volume 3. Records of Josiah Webster, pp. 1–95; records of Rev. E. D. Eldridge; records of Rev. S. Payson Foy; records of Rev. J. Colby; records of Rev. J.A. Ross; Presbyterian Records, pp. 272–286. Copied from original books, 4, 5, 6 located at the First Congregational Church, in Hampton, NH, in the church's Archives.

Haines, Thomas. *Historical Discourse Delivered in the Congregational Church, North Hampton, NH, November 8, 1888 on the 150th Anniversary of the Formation of North Hill Parish.* Boston: Samuel Usher, 1889. [This book is located at the New Hampshire Historical Society Library, Concord, NH.]

"Kingston Church Records - Kingston Deaths and Baptisms of Rev. Joseph Secomb," *The New Hampshire Genealogical Record: An Illustrated Quarterly Magazine*, vol. 5 (January 1908–October

1908). Charles Tibbits, editor and publisher, Dover, NH. [Located at the University of New Hampshire library.]

"Kingston First Church Records 1725–1737," *The New Hampshire Genealogical Record: An Illustrated Quarterly Magazine*, vol. 2 (July 1903–April 1904). Charles Tibbits, editor and publisher, Dover, NH. [Located at the University of New Hampshire library.]

"Record of Congregational Church of Kingston, NH 1739–1792," and also "Church Records of Second Parish in East Kingston, founded 1738," *The New Hampshire Genealogical Record: An Illustrated Quarterly Magazine,* vols. 3 (July 1905–April 1906) and 4 (January 1907–October 1907). Charles Tibbits, editor and publisher, Dover, NH. [Located at the University of New Hampshire Library.]

Moulton, Francis E. *The Records of the Church of Christ in the Town of South Hampton in the Province of New Hampshire in New England, Bound Transcript.* Found in Reverend Mr. Woodbridge Odlin's Book. Exeter, NH, April 11, 1923.

North Hampton Congregational Church Records, vol. 1, 1730–1765. Accessed at New Hampshire State Archives Office of Records Management, Concord, New Hampshire.

Parsons, Langdon Brown. *History of the Town of Rye, New Hampshire from Its Settlement to December 31, 1903.* Rye, NH: Rumford Printing, 1905.

Parsons, William. *Marriages and Baptisms at South Hampton, NH, 1743–1801, Church Records.*

Tallman, Louise. *Baptismal Records of Rye, NH: Adult Church Records from the Congregational Church Records.* Rye, NH, 1980.

The Universalist Society Church Records of Hampton Falls beginning January 2, 1712. Entries by Theophilus Cotton, Pastor of that Church.

Town and County Histories

Arseneault, Judith. *The Vital Records of Kingston, NH 1694–1994.* Baltimore, Maryland: Clearfield Co., 1995.

Bell, Charles H. *History of the Town of Exeter, New Hampshire.* Boston: J.E. Farwell & Co., 1888.

Bouton, Nathaniel. *The History of Concord from its First Grant in 1725 to the Organization of the City Grant in 1853.* Concord, NH: Benning W. Sanborn, 1856.

Brown, Warren. *History of The Town of Hampton Falls, NH from the Time of the First Settlement within Its Borders 1640 until 1900.* Manchester, NH: John B. Clarke Co., 1900.

Brown, Warren. *History of Hampton Falls, NH, Vol. II Containing the Church History and Many Other Things Not Previously Recorded.* Concord, NH: Rumford Press, 1918.

Chase, Benjamin. *History of Old Chester from 1719–1869.* Manchester, NH: Pub. by the author, 1869.

Clark, Susannah J. & Curl, Richard, eds. *The Vital Records of North Hampton, NH, Volume 1. Town Record, 1738–1860, Church records 1739–1900.* Melrose, MA: CV Publishing, 2009.

Coffin, Joshua. *A Sketch of the History of Newbury, Newburyport and West Newbury from 1635–1845.* Boston: Samuel G. Drake, 1845.

Dow, Joseph. *History of the Town of Hampton from Its First Settlement in 1638 to the Autumn of 1892*, vol. 2. Salem, MA: Salem Press Publishing and Printing Co, 1893. 2nd ed., Somersworth, NH: Peter E. Randall Publisher, 1970.

Gordon, George A. *Marriages and Baptisms at South Hampton, NH 1743–1804.* From a MS Copy of the Church Record for Private Distribution. Transcribed by Sweidfeger, Dave. Topsfield, MA: Topsfield Historical Society, 1915.

Hazlett, Charles A. *History of Rockingham County, New Hampshire and Representative Citizen.,* Chicago, IL: Richmond-Arnold Publishing Co., 1915.

Herndon, Ruth Wallis. "To Live After the Manner of an Apprentice: Public Indenture as Social control in Rhode Island 1750–1800." Paper presented at Annual Meeting of American Studies Assn., Boston, November 7, 1993.

Hudson, Charles. *History of the Town of Lexington, Middlesex County, Massachusetts*, vol. 2 Boston: Houghton, Mifflin & Co., Riverside Press, 1913.

Hurd, D. Hamilton. *Merrimack and Sullivan Counties, NH: Containing Life Sketches of Leading Citizens of Merrimack and Sullivan Counties.* Philadelphia: J.W. Lewis & Co., 1885.

Hurd, D. Hamilton. *History of Rockingham and Strafford Counties, NH, with Biographical Sketches of Many of its Pioneers and Prominent Men,* Philadelphia: J.W. Lewis & Co., 1882.

Jones, William Hazlett. *Vital Statistics of North Hampton, New Hampshire, 1742–1942.* Bowie: MD, Heritage Books, Inc. 1999.

Lexington Historical Society Archives, Lexington, MA, 1649 MSS in Ledgers: Book D, June 2, 1739.

Lord, Charles Chase. *Life and Times in Hopkinton, New Hampshire.* Concord, NH: Republica Press Assoc., 1890.

Merrill, Joseph. *The History of Amesbury Including the First Seventeen Years of Salisbury to the Separation in 1654 & Merrimack from its Incorporation 1876.* Haverhill, MA: Press of Franklin P. Stiles, 1880.

"Merrimack and Sullivan Counties, NH." *Biographical Review,* vol. 22.

Page, Roland. *A List of Deaths in Hampton, 1767–1875.* An online record transcribed by Michael Lane can be found at www. hampton.lib.nh.us/hampton/documents/deaths/index.htm.

Parsons, Langdon B. *History of the Town of Rye, New Hampshire from its Discovery and Settlement to December 31, 1903.* Concord, NH: Rumford Printing Co., 1905.

Penhallow, Samuel. North Church Papers, MSO36, Folder 13, Box 8, Collections Account Book Kept by Samuel Penhallow, Portsmouth Athenaum Deposit Collection.

Porthier, Bob, Jr & Lavoie, Ellen. *History of Kingston, New Hampshire 1694–1994: Original Text Compiled in 1969 by Committee of Kingston Improvement and Historical Society.*

Sanborn, George Freeman, Jr., and Melinda Lutz Sanborn. *Vital Records of Hampton, NH to the end of the Year 1900, vol. 2.* Boston: New England Historic Genealogical Society, 1992.

Sawyer, Rev. Roland D. *The History of Kensington, NH 1663–1945, With a Family and Homestead Register of the Pioneer Families,*

Early Settlers and Permanent Citizens of the Town. Farmington, ME: Knowlton & McLeary Co., 1946.

Slaughter, John, Founder. "The Massachusetts Vital Records Project 1620–1988." Vital Records Project, 2005. Transcriptions of the published vital records of early Massachusetts towns from the "Tan Book" series, http://ma-vitalrecords.org/.

Teschek, William. *Epitaphs of the Pine Grove Cemetery,* Recorded 1986, Lane Memorial Library, Hampton, NH.

Vital Records of South Hampton (Town Records), vol.1. Edited and published by the Historical Commission of the South Hampton Friends of the Library, 1970.

Worth, Henry B. *Nantucket Lands and Land Owners.* Nantucket Historical Society, 1901. Internet Archive, http://www.archive.org/details/nantucketlandsla01wort.

Resource Books

Bender, David L. *Puritanism: Opposing Viewpoints.* American History Series, Greenhaven Press, Inc. 1994.

Bly, Antonio T, ed. *Escaping Bondage: A Documentary History of Runaway Slaves in 18th Century New England 1700–1789.* Lanham, MD: Lexington Books, 2012.

Canfield, Mary Grace. *The Valley of the Kedron: The Story of the South Parish, Woodstock, VT.* South Woodstock, VT: Kedron Association, 1940.

Coleman, Elihu. *The Tract on Slavery.* Nantucket, 1729.

Davis, David B. *Inhuman Bondage: The Rise and Fall of Slavery in the New World.* New York: Oxford University Press, 2006.

di Bonaventura, Alegra. *For Adam's Sake: A Family Saga in Colonial New England.* pub 2013.

Dodge, Lawrence G. and Alice C. Dodge. *Puritan Paths from Naumkeag to Piscataqua.* Newburyport Press, 1963.

Earle, Alice Moise. *The Sabbath in Puritan New England.* Williamstown, MA: Corner House Publishing, 1974.

Elliott, Charles Wyllys. *The New England History: from the Discovery of the Continent by the Northmen, AD1776.* New York: Scribner, 1857.

Greene, Lorenzo. *The Negro in Colonial New England 1629–1776.* Washington, NY: Kennikat Press, 1942.

Hymowitz, Carol and Michaele Weissman. *History of Women in America.* New York: Bantam, 1978.

Knoblock, Glen A. *Strong and Brave Fellows, New Hampshire's Black Soldiers and Sailors of the American Revolution, 1775–1784.* Jefferson, North Carolina: McFarland and Co. Inc., 2003.

Lester, Julius. *To Be a Slave.* St. Louis: Turtle Back Books, 2000.

Massachusetts Soldiers and Sailors of the Revolutionary War. Boston, MA: Wright and Potter Printing, 1906. This publication is a compilation of archives.

Melish, Joanne Pope. *Disowning Slavery: Gradual Emancipation and "Race" in New England, 1780–1860.* Ithica: Cornell University Press, 1998.

Moffard, Juliet Haines. *The Devil Made Me Do It - Crime and Punishment in Early New England.* Guilford, CT: Globe Pequot Press, 2012.

Old, Hughes Oliphant. *The Reading and Preaching of the Scriptures in the Worship of the Christian Church,* vol. 5. Grand Rapids, MI: William E. Eerdmans Publishing Co., 2004.

Pierson, William D. *Black Yankees: The Development of an African American Subculture in Eighteenth Century New England.* Amherst: University of MA Press, 1988.

Rapaport, Diane, *The Naked Quaker: True Crimes and Controversies from the Courts of New England.* Beverly, MA: Commonwealth Editions, October 2007.

Rosal, Lorenca Consuelo. *God Save the People: A New Hampshire History.* Orford, NH: Equity Publishing Company, 1988.

Ryan, Kelly A. *Regarding Passion, Sexuality & Patriarchal Rule in Massachusetts, 1700–1830.* New York: Oxford University Press, 2014.

Rosenberg, Chaim M. *The Life and Times of Francis Cabot Lowell 1775–1817.* Lanham, MD: Lexington Books, 2011.

Sammons, Mark J. and Cunningham, Valerie, *Black Portsmouth: Three Centuries of African American Heritage.* Durham, NH: University of New Hampshire Press, 2004.

Sewell, Samuel. *The Selling of Joseph*. Boston: Bartholomew Green and John Allen, 1700.

Tunis, Edward. *Colonial Craftsmen and the Beginnings of American Industry.* Cleveland & NY: The World Publishing Co., 1965.

VanDeventer, David, E. *The Emergence of Provincial New Hampshire 1623–1741.* Baltimore, MD: John Hopkins University Press, 1976.

Zinn, Howard and Anthony Arnove. *Voices of a People's History of the United States.* New York: Seven Stories Press, 2004.

Diaries, Papers, and Articles

Appleton, William, *Selections from the Diaries of William Appleton 1786–1862.* Boston, 1992.

Aykroyd, Elizabeth. *Caesar Long: An African American in 18th Century Hampton.*

Boles, Richard J. *Dividing the Faith: The Rise of Racially Segregated Northern Churches 1730–1850.* A Dissertation Submitted for PhD, May 19, 2013 to George Washington University. Ann Arbor, MI: ProQuest LLC.

Brewster, Charles W. "Brewster's Rambles" 1:155, *Portsmouth Journal of Literature and Politics*, February 1846, Obituary for Dinah Whipple.

Caldwell, Augustine. *Ipswich Antiquarian Papers,* vol. 1–4. Ipswich, MA, 1879–1885. https://archive.org/details/antiquarianpaper00cald.

Cameron, Christopher. "The Puritan Origins of Black Abolitionists in Massachusetts." *The Historical Journal of Massachusetts,* vol. 39. 2011.

Cram, Sarah. "Reminiscences of Hampton Falls, New Hampshire," 2 April 1826. *Exeter Newsletter* as quoted in Quintal, George, Jr. "Patriots of Color: A Peculiar Beauty and Merit," *African Americans and Native Americans at Battle Road & Bunker Hill.* Boston, MA: National Park Service, 2002.

Dixon, David. "Freedom Earned, Equality Denied: Evolving Race Relations in Exeter and Vicinity, 1776–1876." Printed in *Historical New Hampshire,* 61:1, 2007.

Dow, Henry. *Captain Henry Dow's Diary, 1672–1702*. Note: [The original Henry Dow diary is owned by the Dow Chemical Corporation. Three copies were made and one of them is held by Hampton, New Hampshire's Tuck Museum and may be seen there by arrangement.]

Dow, Lucy Ellen. *An Historical Sketch of Hampton, N.H., 1638–1888*. Online resource on the Lane Memorial Library Website, http://www.hampton.lib.nh.us/hampton/history/vignettes/lucydow.htm.

Fuhrer, Mary B., Consulting Historian. *Research for the Re-Interpretation of the Buckman Tavern, Lexington, Massachusetts: Conceptions of Liberty.* Lexington Historical Society, February, 2012.

Fuhrer, Mary B. "Servitude and Slavery in 1775 Lexington." Lexington, MA: The Lexington Historical Society, February 2012.

Gookin, Nathaniel. "Great Earthquake of 1727." A Sermon by Rev. Nathaniel Gookin. Delivered in October/November 1727 in Hampton, NH. Copy owned by First Congregational Church of Hampton.

Hall, Thomas. Interviewed by T. Pat Matthews, September 10, 1937 for WPA Slave Narrative Project, North Carolina Narratives, vol.11, Part 1. Published online by the Library of Congress, Manuscript Division, as part of the *Born in Slavery: Slave narratives from the Federal Writer's Project, 1936–1938.*

Kinney, Charles B., Jr. *Church and State: The Struggle for Separation in New Hampshire 1630–1900.* NY: Columbia University Bureau of Publications, 1955.

Landi, Lauren. *Reading Between the Lines of Slavery: Examining New England Runaway Ads for Evidence of Afro-Yankee Culture.* Pell Scholar Thesis, Salve Regina University, December 2, 2011.

Langdon Papers, Box 1, Folder 2, Series 2. Strawberry Banke Museum, Portsmouth, NH.

Mevers, Frank C. *The Papers of Josiah Barlett.* Hanover, NH: University Press of New England, 1979. Publication of New Hampshire Historical Society, Concord, New Hampshire.

Page, Josiah. *Journal of Epidemic Deaths, 1661–1856*. This journal can be found at Hampton Historical Society Archives, 2009.087.

Penhallow, Samuel. *Collections Account Book*. 17th Century Materials, North Church Papers, MS036, Box 8, Folder 13, 1802–1821. Portsmouth Athenaeum.

Peters, Douglas. *Removing the Heathen: Changing Motives for Indian Slavery in NH*. Concord, NH: NH Historical Society Collection.

Scales, John Longfellow. "The Longfellow Garrison," *The DAR Magazine*, vol. 38:5, May 1911. NY: National Society of the Daughters of the American Revolution.

Shrady, George, and Thomas L. Stedman, "The Conduct of a Surgeon." *Medical Record: A weekly Journal of Medicine and Surgery*, vol.35. New York: William Wood & Company, Trow's Printing and Bookbinding Co., April 20, 1889.

Toppan, Sarah. "Account Book, 1820–1826." Hampton Historical Society Archives 2006.55, Tuck Museum, Hampton, NH.

Tuveson, Erik R. *A People of Color: A Study of Race and Racial Identity in New Hampshire 1750–1825*. Thesis submitted to the University of New Hampshire, May 1995.

Joseph Whipple Diaries, 1731–1736. Accessed in Pre-Revolutionary Diaries Collection of Manuscripts, Massachusetts Historical Society, microfilm, Reel 11, vol.11:14–11:18. Boston, MA.

Wingate, Charles E.L., ed. *Excerpts from the Life and Letters of Paine Wingate – One of the Fathers of the Nation*. Medford, MA: James D. P. Wingate, 1930.

NH State Papers, Probate Records and Other State Papers

Acts and Laws Passed by the General Court of Assembly of His Majesty's Province of New Hampshire in New England. Boston: B. Green, sold by Ebenezer Russel at his shop in Portsmouth, 1716–26. (Original from British Library, digitized October 10, 2014).

Bouton, Nathaniel, and Otis G. Hammond, eds. *New Hampshire Provincial and State Papers*. Manchester: John B. Clarke, printer, 1870.

Calendar of state papers: Colonial Series, American & West Indies, 1677–1680, vol.44, no. 61. London: Gr. Britain Public Record Office, 1896.

Essex County, Massachusetts, 1790 Census.

Essex County Deeds, vol. 54. Patrick Tracy's deed. Found in the Essex Peabody Museum Library, Salem, Massachusetts.

Evans, Helen F. *Abstracts of the Probate Records of Rockingham County, New Hampshire 1771–1799,* vol. 1. Bowie, MD: Heritage Books, Inc. 2000.

Hammond, Otis G., Henry C. Metcalf, et al, eds. *Probate Records of the Province of New Hampshire,* vol. 2–9. Concord, NH: State of New Hampshire, 1867–1943.

_____. *New Hampshire Provincial and State Papers,* vol. 1–40. Concord, NH: State of New Hampshire, 1867–1943.

Hammond, Isaac W., ed. *New Hampshire Revolutionary War Records,* vol. 1. Concord, NH: Parsons B. Cogswell, State Printer, 1885.

_____. *New Hampshire State Papers: Documents relating to Towns in New Hampshire.* Concord, NH: Parsons B. Cogswell, State Printer, 1883.

Hurd, Hamilton D. *History of Rockingham and Strafford Counties, New Hampshire with Biographical Sketches of Many of Its Pioneers and Prominent Men.* Philadelphia, PA: J.W. Lewis and Co., 1882.

Maine Will Abstracts for Residents of York County, Massachusetts, 1640–1760. Probate Office.

Metcalf, Henry Harrison, ed. *Probate Records of the Province of New Hampshire 1718–1740,* vol. 2. State Papers Series, vol. 32. Bristol, NH: R. W. Musgrove, Printer, 1914.

New Hampshire Provincial Deeds, Joseph Locke's deed. Located at the NH Division of Records and Management, State Archives, Concord, NH.

Northwest Ordinance of 1787.

Oesterlin, Pauline Johnson. *Rockingham County, NH Paupers.* Berwyn Heights, MD: Heritage Books, Inc., 1992.

Records and Files of the Quarterly Courts of Essex County, Massachusetts, vol. 4, 1667–1671. Salem, MA: Essex Institute, 1914.

Revolutionary Enlistment, Service, and Pension Records. National Archives: Washington, DC. Microfilm available through subscription to Ancestry.com.

Rockingham County Court Records, "Warning Out" Documents, New Hampshire State Archives, Concord, NH.

"United States Revolutionary War Pension and Bounty-Land Warrant Application Files 1800–1900." National Archives, Department of Veterans Affairs, Washington, DC. Microfilm available through subscription to Ancestry.com.

Worth, Henry B. *Wills and Estates, Part I, 1680–1778: Extracted from Nantucket Lands and Land Owners*. Nantucket, MA: Historical Association, 1901.

Historical Newspapers and Family Papers

Dow, Lucy. *A Sketch of Hampton,* 1899.

Granite Monthly, New Hampshire Magazine, vol. 2, Concord, NH: Granite Monthly Co. 1911.

Independent Chronicle, Boston, Massachusetts.

Jenness, Max L. *Descendants of Job Jenness of Rye, NH.* Rye, NH: Pub. by author, 2008.

Marston Papers 1645–1828, vol. 1, folder 26, December 25, 1761.

"Memoirs and Services of Three Generations of Cilleys." Reprint from the *Courier Gazette.* Rockland, ME: 1909.

New Hampshire Gazette, November 2, 1775 and July 15, 1780.

New England Chronicle (Boston) from Thursday, January 18, to Thursday, January 25, 1776. Runaway slave ads: NH Gazette, 12 April 1771, vol. XV, issue 756, p. 3, Portsmouth.

Genealogical Research

Amos Fortune Family The At-mun Family Tree refers to Amos Fortune's original African family name. Ancestry.com.

Cambridge, Massachusetts, Vital Records to 1850, Marriages. New England Genealogical Society, Boston, 1914.

Dudley, Dean. *History of the Dudley Family*, no. 1. Montrose, MA: Dudley Family, 1886.

Garland, James Gray. *Garland Genealogy: The Descendants of the Northern Branch of Peter Garland, Mariner.* Biddeford, ME: Watson's Illuminator Print, 1897.

Gookin, Frederick William. *Daniel Gookin, 1612–1687. His Life and Letters including the Nansemond Petition, Reintroduction to New England, Residence in Roxbury, and South River Plantation.* Chicago, IL 1912. Ancestry.com.

Jameson, E. O. *The Choates in America 1643–1896, John Choate and His Descendants.* Boston, MA: Alfred Mudge and Son, 1896.

Jones, Thomas E. *Captain Thomas Cromwell 17th C Pirate.* Boston: The New England Historic Genealogical Society, December 1985.

Little, George Thomas, ed. *Genealogical and family History f the State of Maine,* vol. 2. New York: Lewis Historical Publishing Co, 1909.

Noyes, Sybil, Charles T. Libby, and Walter G. Davis. *Genealogical Dictionary of Maine and New Hampshire.* Portland, ME: Genealogical Publishing Company, 1939.

Parsons, Henry A.M. *Descendants of Cornet Joseph Parsons, Springfield 1636 – North Hampton 1635,* vol. 2. New Haven, CT: The Tuttle, Morehouse and Taylor Co., 1920.

Plummer, Steve, J. *The Wheelright Family Story.* Britain: Cloth Wrap Publishing, 2010.

Tibbits, Charles, ed. *NH Genealogical Record: An Illustrated Quarterly,* vol. 5 (January 1908–October 1908). Dover, NH.

Online Research Articles

Benner, Jeffrey. The Ancient Hebrew Research Center, Translations. http://www.ancient-hebrew.org.

Bonham Auction House, December 2006. Edmund Toppan Document from September 20, 1731. https://www.bonhams.com/auctions/14787/lot/449/.

Bouton, Nathaniel. *The History of Concord From its First Grant in 1725 to the Organization of the City Government in 1853,* Chapter VIII, City of Concord, 1765–1775, Miscellaneous Facts and Anecdotes Relative to this Period. Digital Copy can be accessed at: https://books.google.com/

books?id=vKKaM73k8OC&printsec=frontcover&source=gbs_ge_summary_r&cad=0#v=onepage&q&f=true.

Brown, Janice. "New Hampshire: Run-Aways, Desertions & Elopements of the 18th Century." *CowHampshire: New Hampshire's History Blog.* Posted April 7, 2013. www.cowhampshireblog.com/2013/04/07/new-hampshire-run-aways-desertions-elopements-of-the-18th-century/.

Diaz, Brian L., Gentry, Hollis L., Strahan, Jean D., Grundset, Eric G. *Forgotten Patriots - African American and American Indian Patriots in the Revolutionary War.* Commissioned by the Daughters of the American Revolution, 2008. http://www.dar.org/sites/default/files/media/library/DARpublications/Forgotten_Patriots_ISBN-978-1-892237-10-1.pdf.

Dalton, Rodney G. "The First Daltons in the New World," Accessed at: www.daltondatabank.org/chronicles/first_Daltons_In_America.htm.

Dow, Joseph. *King George's War*, 1744–1749. Lane Memorial Excerpts.

Hampton, New Hampshire Town Records, 1798–1825, vol.3, images 109–111. Digital Records can be accessed from the Hampton Historical Society.

Lane, Sarah Hobbs. "General Jonathan Moulton," ca. 1893. Originally appeared in *Fogg's Gazette.* Online, Lane Memorial Library, www.hamptonlib.nh.us/hampton/biog/mo.

Marston, Richard. *Hampton, New Hampshire Area Genealogy,* A database for all residents of Hampton prior to 1900. Copyright 1996–2011. Accessed at: wc.rootsweb.ancestry.com/cgi-bin/igm.cgi?db=Hampton-nh.com.

North Hampton Heritage Commission. "Town of North Hampton Time Line, 1776." A living document of chronologically listed facts about North Hampton, updated every six months. http://www.northhampton-nh.gov/public_documents/northhamptonnh_bcomm/time-l-3.pdf.

Quintal, George, Jr. "Patriots of Color: A Peculiar Beauty and Merit." *African Americans and Native Americans at Battle Road & Bunker Hill.* Boston, MA: National Park Service. https://archive.org/details/patriotsofcolorp00quinrvice, 2002.

Rockingham County, New Hampshire, 1790 State Census of Families with Non-White Members. http://www.rays-place.com/census.htm.

Rockingham County, New Hampshire 1840 Census of Families with Nonwhite members. http://www.rays-place.com/census.htm.

Roth, Mildred. Message dated July 1993 to the Holdredge Family ancestor, Betty Brassington, as recorded in the Landon Family Research Quarterly, vol. 2, Issue 3. Accessed November 2013. http://homepages.rootsweb.ancestry.com/~landon/1993_3/1993_3f.html.

Robinson, J. Dennis. "Agamenticus and Passaconaway," An online review of Sophie Swett's *Stories of Maine* (1899). Article accessed October 2013 through http://www.seacoastnh.com/Places-and-Events/NH-History/agamenticus-and-passaconaway/.

About the Author

DEBORAH KNOWLTON LIVED AS a child on a farm that straddled the town line between Hampton Falls and Exeter, New Hampshire. Educated locally, she attended the University of New Hampshire and Andover Newton Theological School, Newton Center, Massachusetts. She felt the call to ordained ministry in the Exeter Congregational Church and has served parishes over the last thirty-eight years in New Hampshire and Connecticut. She currently serves the First Congregational Church in Hampton. As she read through the ancient church records during the church's 375th anniversary year, she was inspired by what they revealed. Although the history of each parish she served was complex and beautiful, her investigation into Hampton's eighteenth-century African American members felt like discovering neighbors she never knew. *Color Me Included* is her first book.